DATA ANALYSIS AND SAMPLING SIMPLIFIED

A PRACTICAL GUIDE FOR INTERNAL AUDITORS

Donald A. Dickie, PhD

Sponsored by

The Institute of Internal Auditors
Edmonton Chapter

INTERNAL AUDIT
FOUNDATION

Published by the Internal Audit Foundation
1035 Greenwood Blvd., Suite 401
Lake Mary, Florida 32746, USA

Limit of Liability: The Internal Audit Foundation publishes this document for informational and educational purposes and is not a substitute for legal or accounting advice. The Foundation does not provide such advice and makes no warranty as to any legal or accounting results through its publication of this document. When legal or accounting issues arise, professional assistance should be sought and retained.

The IIA's International Professional Practices Framework (IPPF) comprises the full range of existing and developing practice guidance for the profession. The IPPF provides guidance to internal auditors globally and paves the way to world-class internal auditing.

The IIA and the Foundation work in partnership with researchers from around the globe who conduct valuable studies on critical issues affecting today's business world. Much of the content presented in their final reports is a result of Foundation-funded research and prepared as a service to the Foundation and the internal audit profession. Expressed opinions, interpretations, or points of view represent a consensus of the researchers and do not necessarily reflect or represent the official position or policies of The IIA or the Foundation.

ISBN-13: 978-1-63454-061-2
23 22 21 20 19   1 2 3 4 5 6

CONTENTS

Introduction to Analytical Procedures

Analytical Procedures

Selecting Items for Testing to Obtain Audit Evidence

LIST OF TABLES

LIST OF FIGURES

PREFACE

In the fall of 2017, the Internal Audit Foundation asked me to write a book on data analysis and sampling. Having taught these courses for just over 15 years and never having written a book (several theses don't count), I considered this to be a worthwhile challenge—somewhat tedious but doable. And then a colleague told me about the State of Oklahoma data set and I was reminded why I left a potential career in academia and instead moved into industry.

There is something about live data that draws out the explorer, the quest for the unknown. The tediousness disappeared and the excitement returned—though many of my closer friends found me quite delusional. I alternated between writing chapters and performing analysis. And I ran into many of the challenges that auditors frequently face when confronted with live data. It was as much an eye opener (since I had forgotten those early years of diving into data) as it was a joy to reinvigorate some of those dormant skills.

I remember what it's like to face that first large data set on the computer screen wondering how to proceed. My hope is that readers will find this book helpful as they take on the challenges that come with data analysis and sampling.

ACKNOWLEDGMENTS

Live data was used from the State of Oklahoma P-Card transactions for 2011–2012 and 2012–2013 to demonstrate the various analytical procedures. I am forever grateful to the government employees of the State of Oklahoma who allowed their expenditure data to be published online, thus allowing internal auditors an opportunity to practice their analytical skills on live data. Please note that the anomalies that were discovered in the data are being used to illustrate specific analytic techniques that internal auditors will be able to use to identify high-risk areas in business entities. *Under no circumstances should it be implied that the discovered anomalies are indications of anything other than appropriately approved and valid transactions.*

ABOUT THE AUTHOR

Donald A. Dickie, PhD, is a professional statistician who spent about a third of his career in internal auditing and the remainder in various senior executive roles with one of Canada's largest crown corporations, thus on the receiving end as a client of internal auditors. Since 2003, he has developed and taught seminars in data analysis and sampling specifically designed for internal auditors within the federal governments of Canada and the United States as well as private sector companies throughout North America. As president of D. A. Dickie Inc., he has consulting clients within Canada and the United States and appears in court as an expert witness for sampling issues raised in forensic auditing.

INTRODUCTION TO
ANALYTICAL PROCEDURES

Chapter 1

INTRODUCTION

About This Book

This is a book about data—about how to reduce large data sets down to the critical few high-risk subsets and how to select items or transactions for testing. It is my hope that this book will help auditors when they are confronted with very large data sets that contain hundreds of millions of items. Though these data sets will contain both numeric, alphanumeric, and text data, the various data fields are driven by the underlying financial model of the business entity. In other words, there is an association between the various fields in the data set and the revenue or cost activities of the business entity. More and more business entities are moving into what has been termed "big data," which includes the above and the content of social media. Social media data is not something that statistical analysis can address, though the cutting-edge developers of artificial intelligence are using complex mathematical models to sift through social media data in relation to market and business trends.

This book does not address the inclusion of social media in the data, but it does deal with large data sets that are becoming more and more common in the internal audit community. Most of the book is devoted to data analysis, or what is more formally described as analytical procedures. This was a conscious choice due to the lack of clear guidance about *how* to perform the various techniques that are encompassed within analytical procedures. The analytical procedures are broken down into frequency analysis and time series analysis. Each contains a graphical component and a statistical metric component as well as data presented in a tabular format.

The language—Selecting Items for Testing—was specifically adopted from the Public Accounting Oversight Board's Auditing Standard 1105, Audit Evidence (December 2010). Selecting Items for Testing to Obtain Audit Evidence is divided into three distinct sections: Selecting All Items, Selecting Specific Items, and Audit (Random) Sampling. Auditing Standard 1105 was deliberately selected because of the simplicity of the language that describes the various methods used to select items for testing.

IIA Standard 2320 – Analysis and Evaluation also moves in a direction of simplifying the language around sampling:

> "Internal auditors may test a complete population or a representative sample of information. If they choose to select a sample, they are responsible for applying methods to assure that the sample selected represents the whole population and/or time period to which the results will be generalized. The use of CAATs may enable the analysis of an entire population of information, rather than just a sample." (IIA Standard 2320, Implementation Guide)

This book endeavours to cover the major activities that arise from the subdivision, selection, and analysis of data. Some of these activities interact with other more formal audit activities such as the engagement-level risk assessment. Others are considered more purely statistical in nature. However, all of the activities described in this book adhere to risk-based auditing and can be tailored to align with an audit objective and fit within a defined audit scope. The results of these activities will be found in the audit report, documented in the audit working papers, and considered as evidence to support the audit's findings. The flow of the activities addressed in this book are illustrated in **figure 1-1**.

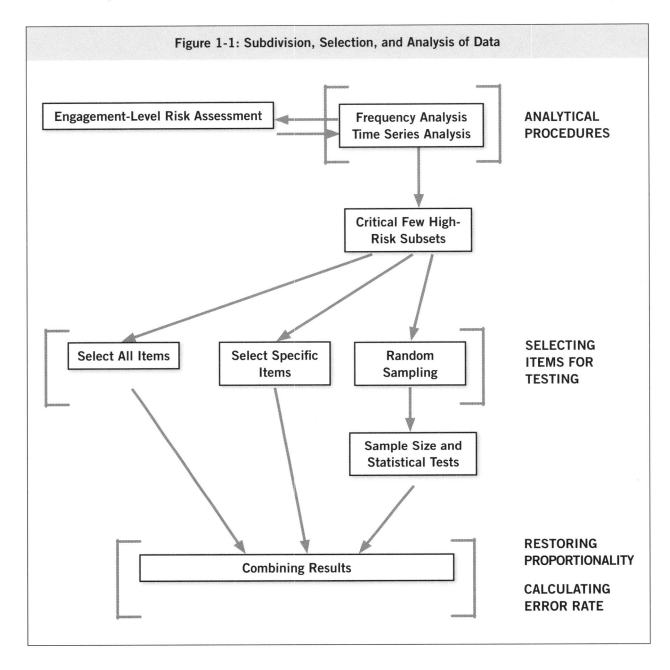

Figure 1-1: Subdivision, Selection, and Analysis of Data

Case Study Data and Analytical Procedures

The demonstration of analytical techniques depends on having a source of data that can be manipulated and examined. Some authors prefer to fabricate the data to demonstrate different types of findings. It was a deliberate choice to use live data to demonstrate the various analytical techniques. The use of live data was preferred because not only can the techniques be demonstrated, but the very common problems that auditors face when they confront live data are also apparent. Many of these problems will not be seen in fabricated data because the data has been structured to demonstrate a specific technique or finding. The disadvantage of using live data is that the risk assessment information that would normally be associated with this data is not available. This means that the reader must accept some fairly generic assumptions about the nature of the risk in the case studies. I believe that the advantages of live data far outweigh the disadvantage of making some relatively generic assumptions about risk.

The majority of the case studies in this book rely on the data published by the State of Oklahoma. The data is composed of the State of Oklahoma's P-Card transactions for the years 2011–2012 and 2012–2013. There are just over 400,000 transactions in each of the two fiscal years, which means this data set is on the small side given the size of current data sets that reside in the millions and hundreds of millions of transactions. However, it is large enough to require analytical techniques.

The analytical procedures encompass frequency analysis and time series or trend analysis. The theory supporting these two analytic techniques is described in detail in chapters 4 and 6 respectively. Though the techniques differ, the steps followed in each analytical technique are the same and are described in **figure 1-2**.

Figure 1-2: The Steps Involved in Analytical Procedures

Step 1 – Become Familiar with the Data

- Understand the columns and the nature of the data contained in each column.
- Pay particular attention to what is contained in the columns since this will form the basis of probing questions during the engagement-level risk assessment.

Step 2 – Understand the Market Segment and Conditions Affecting the Market

- Consider a frequency distribution and a time series distribution at the highest level (typically the complete data set).
- Identify abnormalities in the frequency and time series distributions and relate those abnormalities to changes in the market conditions. This step is important so that abnormalities driven by the market are not confused with abnormalities driven by high-risk factors.

Step 3 – Validate the Benchmark Data Set

- The validation is done with both the frequency analysis and time series analysis and for both internal and external benchmarks.
- The benchmark data set should display a similar shape to what is expected in the market as a whole.

Figure 1-2: The Steps Involved in Analytical Procedures (continued)
Step 4 – Compare the Data Set of Concern to the Internal Benchmark
• Perform frequency and time series analyses comparing the data set of concern to the internal benchmark.
Step 5 – Compare the Data Set of Concern to the External Benchmark
• Perform frequency and time series analyses comparing the data set of concern to the external benchmark.
Step 6 – Validate Identified Abnormalities in the Data Set of Concern with Management
• Once abnormalities have been identified, validate the findings with management to ensure that they are driven by high-risk factors and not something such as a change in procedures or market conditions.
Step 7– Compare the Results of Both Frequency and Time Series Analysis
• Are the results consistent?   • Ensure the subsets are mutually exclusive.   • Prioritize the subsets based on risk/impact to the business entity.

Chapters 5 and 7 address the case studies for frequency analysis and time series analysis respectively. Each of the analytic techniques follow the steps described above. It was a conscious choice to standardize the steps for ease of understanding. The analysis described in these chapters looks at the data from all perspectives and shows graphs and tables that depict the findings.

In all likelihood, there are more analyses performed in the case studies than are necessary in a typical audit. However, the intent was to demonstrate all possible perspectives on the data. It is my hope that readers of this book will consider taking a look at the State of Oklahoma data and replicate the findings illustrated in the applicable chapters.

Proportionality and Risk-Based Auditing

Proportionality is a sampling characteristic used when the population is composed of several subgroups that are vastly different in size. Often referred to as probability proportional to size (PPS) or proportional sampling, this sampling strategy ensures that the number of items from each subgroup is determined by the size of the subset relative to the entire population.

However, items or transactions viewed as high risk form a very small proportion of the total population, though in absolute numbers they may be quite large. If a proportional sampling strategy is used to select items, then the high-risk subset will have proportionally fewer items selected. Few sources describe the relationship between risk-based auditing and proportionality. The Organization for the Economic Co-operation and Development (OECD) is a unique forum where governments work together to address the economic, social, and environmental challenges of globalization. The quote listed below comes from their 2014 Best Practice Principles for Regulatory Policy.

"**Risk focus and proportionality:** Enforcement needs to be risk-based and proportionate: the frequency of inspections and the resources employed should be proportional to the level of risk and enforcement actions should be aiming at reducing the actual risk posed by infractions." [OECD (2014), Regulatory Enforcement and Inspections, OECD Best Practice Principles for Regulatory Policy, OECD Publishing, p. 14.]

OECD best practice specifically states that the frequency of inspections (sample size) and the resources employed (to collect all types of evidence) should be proportional to the risk level. In other words, high-risk subsets of concern should have larger sample sizes attached to them and more effort (from the audit team, inspectors, etc.) applied to them. The OECD article goes on to state that the enforcement actions (recommendations and corresponding corrective actions by management) should be aimed at reducing the actual risk levels posed by the infractions. In other words, the intent of risk-based inspections is to bring down the inherent and residual risk levels in the business entity.

Though the OECD article focuses on the regulatory environment, there are similarities between sampling strategies used in regulatory inspections and those used in internal auditing. Of primary concern to both areas is the concept of risk and the need to reduce risk to an acceptable level. When risk is not addressed adequately, business entities may lose millions or billions of dollars. In the regulatory environment, particularly in such areas as rail and airline safety, missing key high-risk entities (such as train cars or airplanes) results in environmental impacts, injury, and quite possibly fatalities.

Auditors should never feel constrained by proportionality. In fact, moving away from proportionality allows them the freedom to allocate sample size based on risk levels rather than the size of the underlying population subsets. As will be seen in chapter 11, "Combining Results," proportionality can always be restored using weighted averages. The potential advantages of moving away from proportionality are counterbalanced by the auditors' need to examine everything. In the past, examining high-risk items and using proportional designs was possible with smaller populations. Today, population sizes have moved into the hundreds of millions of items. Attempting to examine everything through the use of a finite sample size that is distributed proportionally means that the majority of the sample size will be allocated to low-risk subsets.

Case Study—Proportionality and Sample Size

Given the intent of risk-based auditing, all audits begin with a risk focus. However, the risk-focus intent is not always continued throughout the audit, especially when allocating sample size. Consider the following example.

Table 1-1 lists the frequency of the P-Card expenditures for the 2012–2013 fiscal year for the State of Oklahoma.

Table 1-1: State of Oklahoma, P-Card Transactions 2012–2013	
Dollar Intervals	**Frequency**
-$100,000 to -$75,000	2
-$75,001 to -50,000	1
-$50,001 to -$25,000	4

Table 1-1: State of Oklahoma, P-Card Transactions 2012–2013 (continued)	
-$25,001 to -0.01	14,970
$0.01 to $25,000	426,474
$25,001 to $50,000	203
$50,001 to $75,000	57
$75,001 to $100,000	45
$100,001 to $125,000	9
$125,001 to $150,000	2
$150,001 to $175,000	1
$175,001 to $200,000	2
$2225,001 to $250,000	2
$250,001 to $275,000	1
$375,001 to $400,000	1
$575,001 to $600,000	1
$775,001 to $800,000	1
$875,001 to $900,000	1
$1,175,001 to $1,200,000	1
$1,600,001 to $1,625,000	1
$1,750,001 to $1,775,000	2
	441,781

Imagine performing an audit of the P-Card transactions. Consider for the sake of simplicity those transactions less than 0 (negative values—credits) are not considered within scope of this audit. Removing those transactions leaves the following within scope of the audit (see **table 1-2**).

Further suppose that there are sufficient resources to examine a sample size of 70 transactions. How would sample size be allocated across the various dollar intervals? There are several alternatives, the most popular being allocating sample size proportionally based on subpopulation (dollar interval) frequency or size. However, in this case, given the large number of transactions under $25,000 (roughly 99% of the population), allocating sample size based solely on subpopulation size severely limits the coverage of the remaining intervals. The modified proportional to population size limits the allocation of 50 transactions to the first interval and allocates the remaining 20 proportionally to the remaining intervals.

Table 1-2: State of Oklahoma, P-Card Transactions 2012–2013, Negative Transactions (Credits) Removed	
Dollar Intervals	**Frequency**
$0.01 to $25,000	426,474
$25,001 to $50,000	203
$50,001 to $75,000	57
$75,001 to $100,000	45
Over $100,000	25
	426,804

Both sample size allocations in **table 1-3** rely upon proportionality either in total or to some extent. The first example would occur if the auditor chose not to subdivide the population of 426,804 transactions into smaller subsets and instead simply took one large random sample of 70 transactions from the total population. In all likelihood, the resulting random sample would be composed of 69 transactions less than $25,000 and 1 transaction greater than $25,000. The second column mildly deviates from proportionality by allocating 50 items to the subset less than $25,000 and the remaining 20 proportionally to the other four subsets.

Table 1-3: State of Oklahoma, P-Card Transactions 2012–2013, Probability Proportional to Population Size			
Dollar Intervals	**Frequency**	**Proportional to Population Size**	**Modified Proportional to Population Size**
$0.01 to $25,000	426,474	69	50
$25,001 to $50,000	203	1	12
$50,001 to $75,000	57	0	4
$75,001 to $100,000	45	0	3
Over $100,000	25	0	1
	426,804		

The question remains whether either of these two designs is risk based. The OECD best practice states that the frequency of inspections should be proportional to risk level. If dollar value is considered an indicator of risk, then high-dollar transactions would be considered to be the most risky. In the above example, the transactions exceeding $100,000 (the most risky) account for less than 2% of the total sample size. A proportional allocation of sample size (if the desire is to be risk based) is appropriate when risk is proportional to frequency or subpopulation size (i.e., the number of transactions in any given subset).

A risk-based sample size allocation departs from proportional to population size. Unfortunately, there is no easy calculation to determine how to allocate sample size. The decision rests with the auditors and their professional assessment of the nature and magnitude of the risks in each subpopulation. Several possible scenarios are listed in **table 1-4**, all of which could be useful depending on the magnitude of the risks involved.

Table 1-4: State of Oklahoma, P-Card Transactions 2012–2013, Probability Proportional to Risk Level					
Dollar Intervals	Frequency	Proportional to Level of Risk	Proportional to Level of Risk	Proportional to Level of Risk	Proportional to Level of Risk
$0.01 to $25,000	426,474	0	5	0	70
$25,001 to $50,000	203	10	10	25	0
$50,001 to $75,000	57	15	15	45	0
$75,001 to $100,000	45	20	15	0	0
Over $100,000	25	25	25	0	0
TOTAL	426,804	70	70	70	70

Consider the first example in **table 1-4**. The focus in the first example is only on those transactions greater than $25,000, with higher sample sizes being used in the higher dollar value transactions. Given that the risk is the greatest with those transactions exceeding $100,000, all 25 transactions were examined.

The second example still focuses on the high-dollar transactions but spreads out into those transactions less than $25,000. This example most commonly reflects those sample designs where the auditors feel the need to cover everything. However, they must ask themselves whether the sample size of five provides any value on a subpopulation of more than 426,000 transactions.

The third example considers the scenario where the auditors verified through other means that the 70 transactions greater than $75,000 were low risk (for example, assume that these transactions followed a different approval process and were heavily scrutinized). The auditors also chose to look at the transactions less than $25,000 through a process walkthrough, interviews with management, and running of generic and customized scripts to detect any fraudulent activity. This leaves two subdivisions in which the auditors will focus their efforts.

The final example is based on the auditors' assessment that the risk level for the transactions above $25,000 is low. This decision would be typical in a situation where those expenses were subjected to a different process or more scrutiny and approvals. The auditors would still need to verify that the key controls were still effective for transactions exceeding $25,000. In this case, the auditors' effort would be focused on the 426,804 transactions less than $25,000. The subpopulation size is still excessively large, forcing the auditors to subdivide these transactions based on risk. Note that the process would be repeated a second time to narrow down the number of subdivisions to the critical few high-risk subsets.

Each of four examples is viable with both advantages and disadvantages. The auditors must choose where to focus their efforts based on their professional assessment of risk. The major theme across all of the examples is that the auditors must understand the risk framework relative to the business entity and bring the engagement-level risk assessment into the data analysis. Risk-based auditing is more than linking the risk management processes of the business entity to internal audit's annual plan. Risk-based auditing must be a cornerstone at the engagement level as well.

One of the outcomes of a risk-based approach is that examination of transactions based on either subdivision or sampling is confined to only those subsets deemed to be high risk. However, the remaining subsets (medium and low risk) cannot be ignored. This would result in a change of scope of the audit, which typically requires audit committee and audit management approval. Consequently, the lower risk subsets are examined using the remaining evidence collection methods (observation, inquiry, confirmation, inspection, analytical procedures, recalculation and re-performance). In general, these methods are less resource intensive than the various examination of transaction strategies.

Summary – What's Important

- The analytical procedures yield the critical few high-risk subsets.

- Selecting items for testing (selecting all items, selecting specific items, and random sampling), if driven by risk-based auditing, will distort proportionality.

- The amount of resourcing, the sample size, the quantity of evidence—in short, the effort—should be proportional to the risk level.

- Allocating sample size based on population size—probability proportional to size (PPS)—negates the impact of risk *unless* risk is proportional to frequency or population size.

- Departing from proportional to population size is necessary whenever risk is *not* proportional to population size.

- Restoring proportionality and calculating individual subset and overall error rates or noncompliance rates is necessary for reporting.

ANALYTICAL PROCEDURES

Chapter 2

RISK ASSESSMENT AND THE DATA SET

Though the overall population error rate is of interest, of greater interest are the subsets of the population with very large error rates that are not compliant, evade controls, or present specific risks to the business entity. The probability of finding a group of transactions that does not have an error rate close to the population error rate is relatively small and directly proportional to the number of transactions in that specific group. Consider 1,000 transactions that are problematic, such as being the result of corporate fraud. By itself, 1,000 transactions are considered to be quite large. However, in a population of 2,000,000 transactions, they constitute only .05% of the total. If the population is decreased to 500,000, the proportion of fraudulent transactions increases to .2%. The chances of finding these transactions in a random sample drawn from the whole population is extremely low. Increasing the sample size, even if the audit department could afford the cost, is not a viable solution over the long term since data sets are continuing to grow in size. Ten years ago, a data set of a million transactions was considered large. In today's world, large data sets number in the hundreds of millions.

Risk Assessment

Early in the audit, an engagement-level risk assessment is performed. The intent of this chapter is not to recommend a specific risk assessment methodology. There are many viable and well-respected risk assessments in use in the auditing community. However, for subdivision based on risk to be successful, the risk assessment must be driven down to a lower level than the business entity as a whole and be integrated with the analytical procedures.

At the engagement level, the relevant risks are identified and ranked, and those considered to be within the scope of the engagement are carried forward into the audit. It is at this point where integration with the analytical procedures takes place.

Data Sets

Data sets are composed of columns and rows. The rows can number from the hundreds up to the millions and represent the size of the data set. The columns, on the other hand, are relatively stable and few in number. Typically there are about 15 to 30 columns of data. In instances where the data is from a survey type instrument (a tool that collects multiple fields of information), the number of columns may be very high. However, for the purposes of an audit, the number of relevant columns within scope of a particular engagement is relatively small. The columns can contain data of three different formats. Some will contain exclusively text data such as an employee name, management level, facility name, etc. Others will contain alphanumeric content such as dates, addresses, account or client codes, etc. And there will be those that contain solely numerical data such as financial quantities (dollars), frequencies or totals, durations, etc.

The columns are vastly more important than the rows because they provide the ability to subdivide the population into smaller subsets. Additionally, the numerical columns can be subjected to statistical analysis such as frequency analysis, calculations of central tendency, time series analysis, and calculations of correlations. Operational or process audits, control audits, compliance audits, or financial audits all produce numerical data and can therefore be subjected to data analysis. Though the nature of the numerical data is very different across the different audits, the manner in which the numerical data is treated statistically remains the same.

The challenge facing the auditor is how to integrate the knowledge from the data set into the risk assessment. The first step is to understand the nature of the columns and the data contained in the columns. Acquire an electronic copy of the first 100 rows of the data set and *all* columns. Review the column label and the data listed in the column in order to understand what the column heading is referring to and the nature of the data associated with the column heading. Next, select those columns that are clearly within scope of the audit. The auditor must understand what is contained in each column and the nature of the labels and language used to describe the columns.

Integrating the Engagement-Level Risk Assessment and the Data Set

Traditionally, the risk assessment is performed early in the planning phase of the audit and is typically composed of a series of meetings with senior management and stakeholders. During the meeting, if a risk is identified with a high level of impact and likelihood and a low ability to mitigate, the auditor should probe to determine more precise information. It is at this point that the auditor should ask questions using the language of the columns (column headers, column content) to determine precisely where the risk is located. In other words, the auditor should probe about which facility, which organizational unit, which customers, etc.—knowing that the facility name, organizational unit, and customer name are included in the data set. It is critical that the risk assessment be pushed down to the lowest level so that analytical procedures can be employed.

The nature of traditional risk assessment has slightly changed, though the content of the risk assessment remains essentially the same. Integrating the risk assessment with the analytical procedures moves the risk assessment from a one-time occurrence to something that is more cyclical in nature. **Figure 2-1** illustrates the steps integrating the risk assessment with the analytical procedures.

Note the interactive nature of the process. Auditors use their understanding of the data set to probe during the risk assessment. The results of the probing lead to subdivision of the data set and the consequent application of the analytical procedures. If senior management and the stakeholders have provided accurate information, the analytical procedures will identify where the subcomponent in question deviates from what is expected. Once that deviation has been identified, the auditor validates the finding with senior management, stakeholders, and perhaps line management responsible for the data that deviates from what would be expected. Ideally, each identified high risk should lead to a subcomponent that can be identified and subjected to the analytical procedures.

It is important to understand that the success of the analytical procedures relies heavily on the risk assessment providing high-risk subsets. If the risk assessment is not taken down to the lowest level in the data, then the subdivision will be meaningless and the subsequent analytical procedures doomed to failure.

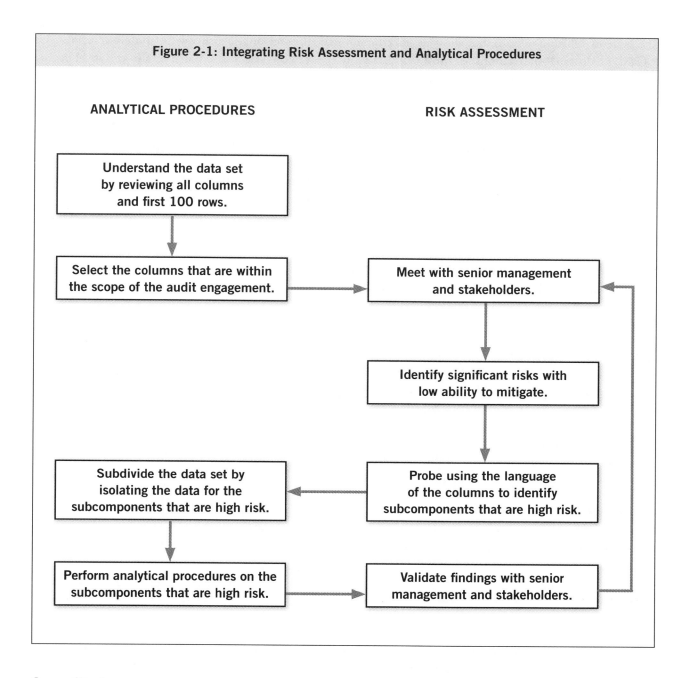

Figure 2-1: Integrating Risk Assessment and Analytical Procedures

ANALYTICAL PROCEDURES

RISK ASSESSMENT

Understand the data set by reviewing all columns and first 100 rows.

Select the columns that are within the scope of the audit engagement.

Meet with senior management and stakeholders.

Identify significant risks with low ability to mitigate.

Subdivide the data set by isolating the data for the subcomponents that are high risk.

Probe using the language of the columns to identify subcomponents that are high risk.

Perform analytical procedures on the subcomponents that are high risk.

Validate findings with senior management and stakeholders.

Case Study

Become Familiar with the Data Set

The following is an example of how an auditor would become familiar with a data set. For some readers, this might appear to be an unnecessary step. However, if you are not familiar with the data, then you cannot structure probing questions that provide direction for subdivision of the data set.

The State of Oklahoma publishes all of its government expenditures online available for public scrutiny. The P-Card (credit card) transactions for fiscal year 2012–2013 have been selected to illustrate the analytical procedures. There are 441,781 transactions listed for the 2012–2013 fiscal year accounting for a total dollar value of $181,785,291.20.

At this point in understanding the data, the sort function in Excel is the auditor's best friend. Sorting the various columns in both directions and then scanning what is in the column provides valuable information.

The following 11 columns are contained in the data set. When first examining the data set, it is a good idea to have the first 100 rows downloaded so that the format of the data contained in each column can be examined if the data set is extremely large or if it takes significant time to get access to the data set. Otherwise, download it into Excel and use the sort function.

Year Month: This column contains numerical data that are six digits in length. The first four digits correspond to the year and the last two digits to the month. The data ranges from 201207 (July 2012) to 201306 (June 2013).

Agency Number: The column contains numerical data with either four or five digits. There are 116 unique codes.

Agency Name: The column contains text data. There are 121 unique names. There are several instances where the same agency code has two different agency names attached to it. In all cases but one, it appears that the different agency names are simply due to different spellings. The one exception is the Office of Management and Enterprise Services and Office of State Finance.

Cardholder Last Name: This column contains both text and numeric data (not alphanumeric, since the numeric and text are in different rows). Some of the text appears to be the family name of an individual and others the name of a company. The numeric data contains numbers that range from 1,000 to 88,000 with only 18 different values.

Cardholder First Name: This column contains text data and numeric data (not alphanumeric data). Those with single digit numeric values are associated with the cardholder last name that also contains numeric data. The remaining data contains the first initial of the first name. Note that some last names have several different first initials associated with them.

Description: This column contains numeric data, text data, and alphanumeric data. There are 87,823 different descriptions.

Amount: This column contains numeric data (dollar format) with both negative (credits) and positive values (expenditures). The highest dollar value is $1,764,140.27 and the lowest dollar value (the largest credit) is -$99,999.99.

Vendor: This column contains text data, numeric data, and alphanumeric data. There are 90,728 different vendor names/codes.

Transaction Date: This column contains alphanumeric data that includes day, month, and year, and in some cases, time (hours, minutes, seconds). It was also discovered that some of this data is stored in a numeric format (date format) and some in a text format, making it unsuitable for analysis in Excel. Consequently, this column was reconfigured to a simple date format for analysis.

Posting Date: This column contains alphanumeric data that includes day, month, and year, and in some cases, time (hours, minutes, seconds). It was also discovered that some of this data is stored in a numeric format (date format) and some in a text format, making it unsuitable for analysis in Excel. This column was not reconfigured because the transaction date would provide sufficient data for time series analysis.

Merchant Category Code (MCC): This column contains text data. There are 496 different codes, including blanks.

At this point, the auditor has already bounded the population so that it is consistent with the scope of the audit. The next step requires the auditor to unleash his/her natural curiosity in order to explore the data. The review of the data is done prior to the risk assessment and, although it should not be constrained by risk, it should consider the reasonableness of various findings.

There are 121 different agencies that submitted P-Card transactions in the State of Oklahoma during the fiscal year 2012–2013. Of those agencies, 12 of them account for 80.6% of the total number of transactions (see **table 2-1**).

Table 2-1: State of Oklahoma 2012–2013, Agency and Total Frequency	
Agency Name	**Frequency**
Oklahoma State University	116,179
University of Oklahoma	81,711
University of Oklahoma Health Sciences Center	57,942
Department of Corrections	22,394
Department of Transportation	15,756
Department of Tourism and Recreation	15,724
Grand River Dam Authority	9,749
Department of Rehabilitation Services	8,628
Southwestern Oklahoma State University	7,538
Department of Veterans Affairs	7,483
Office of Management and Enterprise Services*	7,038
Mental Health and Substance Abuse Services	5,959

*Note that this is a combined total for the Office of Management and Enterprise Services and the Office of State Finance.

Now consider including the dollar amount of the transactions. The top 12 spending agencies account for 84.1% of the total P-Card expenditures and are listed in **table 2-2**.

Table 2-2: State of Oklahoma 2012–2013, Agency and Total Dollar Amount	
Agency Name	**Total Dollar Amount**
Oklahoma State University	$35,211,579.45
University of Oklahoma	$30,527,905.31
University of Oklahoma Health Sciences Center	$22,603,378.77
Grand River Dam Authority	$17,640,224.57
Department of Corrections	$14,284,326.11
Department of Transportation	$11,570,911.87
Department of Tourism and Recreation	$5,277,328.81
Department of Veterans Affairs	$3,779,556.79
Office of Management and Enterprise Services*	$3,612,959.16
Oklahoma Military Department	$3,363,247.3
Department of Rehabilitation Services	$2,624,413.99
State Department of Health	$2,359,363.73

*Note that this is a combined total for the Office of Management and Enterprise Services and the Office of State Finance.

However, the top 12 based on frequency are not the same as the top 12 based on total dollar value. The State Department of Health and the Office of Management and Enterprise Services have moved into the 11th and 12th position. Mental Health and Substance Abuse and Southwestern Oklahoma State University have dropped out of the top 12. The top three with respect to total dollar value are state universities and account for 48.6% of the total expenses for the State of Oklahoma.

The P-Card data contains a fair amount of transactions from educational institutions. Of the total number of P-Card transactions, 64% belong to educational institutions. With respect to the total dollar value, 53% of the total dollar amount was spent by educational institutions. **Table 2-3** lists the total frequency and dollar amount for the 16 Oklahoma institutions.

Table 2-3: State of Oklahoma, Frequency and Dollar Amount of P-Card Transactions for Educational Institutions 2012–2013		
Educational Institutions	**Total Frequency**	**Total Dollar Amount**
Oklahoma State University	116,179	$35,211,579.45
University of Oklahoma	81,711	$30,527,905.31
University of Oklahoma Health Sciences Center	57,942	$22,603,378.77

Table 2-3: State of Oklahoma, Frequency and Dollar Amount of P-Card Transactions for Educational Institutions 2012–2013 (continued)		
Southwestern Oklahoma State University	7,538	$1,414,258.76
Oklahoma Panhandle State University	4,486	$734,321.94
Tulsa Community College	4,389	$2,055,347.84
Oklahoma Department of Career and Technology Education	3,739	$1,682,948.83
Redlands Community College	2,329	$737,378.89
Langston University	1,654	$445,964.42
Eastern Oklahoma State College	1,344	$325,048.2
Oklahoma City Community College	802	$349,226.26
Rose State College	695	$219,007.67
Northeastern Oklahoma A&M College	503	$103,592.53
University of Science and Arts of Oklahoma	459	$135,567.07
Oklahoma School of Science & Math	217	$104,468.92
Regional University System of Oklahoma	207	$43,623.34
TOTAL	284,194	$96,693,618.2

The three institutions with the largest number of P-Card transactions are Oklahoma State University, University of Oklahoma, and University of Oklahoma Health Sciences Center. They account for 90% of the transactions and 91% of the total dollars with respect to all educational institutions in the state. Relative to the State of Oklahoma, the three institutions account for 58% of the total number of transactions and 48.6% of the total dollar value.

Use Probing Questions in the Risk Assessment

As the auditor works through the risk assessment, management will provide pieces of information about various parts of the organization. It is at this point that the auditor begins to ask probing questions, which are driven by the nature of the columns in the data set. In this way, the assessment of risk is linked to the analytical procedures. Let's assume that management's interest is in the credit card transactions for the various educational institutions, particularly the largest institutions. Once this is apparent, the auditor would begin to probe with much more specific questions that incorporate the language from various columns. For example:

Year Month: Is there a specific month that behaves differently with respect to credit card transactions (such as more than expected or less than expected)? Is there a month that you view to be higher risk? Why?

Agency Name: Is there a specific educational institution that you believe is a greater risk? The University of Oklahoma Health Sciences Center has some very large expenditures but only 3,600 students. Even though this faculty trains all of the medical professionals, are the expenditures in line with its mandate?

Cardholder Last Name: Do you know of any employees who have had credit card problems in the past? These employees have authorized some very large expenditures. Is this reasonable given their position and responsibilities?

Description: There have been several large value transactions that are listed as payment adjustments from vendors such as Staples. Do you consider these to be reasonable?

Amount: There are 680 transactions that exceed $5,000, which according to corporate policy is the maximum expenditure. Are these transactions reasonable?

Vendor: Is there a specific vendor that appears to be doing more business than one would expect at a university?

The purpose of these questions is to move the risk information down to a more granular level and use it to subdivide the data into potentially high-risk subsets. Once the data has been subdivided based on risk, analytical procedures can be applied.

After the first series of risk assessment interviews, the auditor should have sufficient information to be able to subdivide the population and isolate one or more high-risk subsets. For the Oklahoma State data, these subsets might be a specific agency, vendor, or employee. They may also be transactions exceeding a specific dollar value or occurring in a specific time frame. Some of the concerns raised by management may be simply supposition; others may have their basis in actual evidence and experience. The challenge for the auditor is to identify which are supposition and which are valid high-risk subsets that need to be pursued. To do that, the auditor needs a benchmark data set.

Summary – What's Important

- The probability of finding a high-risk subset in a large data set through the use of a random sample drawn from the entire population is very low, which is why subdivision is an essential tool for auditors. The population needs to be reduced to a limited number of high-risk subsets.

- The success of the analytical procedures is totally dependent on the meaningfulness of the subdivision.

- For the subdivision to be meaningful, it must be driven by risk, which means that the success of the subdivision is totally dependent on the engagement-level risk assessment.

Case Study

- Understand the columns of data, which includes understanding what is in the columns, such as units, format, totals, and partitions (i.e., the 80/20 rule).

- Integrate the language of columns into the risk assessment. This means the risk assessment process is begun after there is an understanding of the columns of the data set.

- Use the responses to the risk assessment to subdivide the data set into high-risk subsets.

Chapter 3

SELECTING A BENCHMARK DATA SET

Once a high-risk subset has been identified as a result of the risk assessment, the auditor is left with the question, "How does one know whether the individual subset identified from the risk assessment is actually high risk or not?" In case of fraudulent or unusual transactions, the selection criteria provides sufficient evidence to at least begin the investigative process. But what about subsets that have hundreds of thousands or millions of transactions?

Statistical procedures, in and of themselves, cannot answer the question as to whether the identified subset is high risk or not. Rather, statistical procedures are used to compare two or more sets of numbers to see if they are similar or different. The first step in this process is selecting a benchmark data set that the auditor can trust is low risk. Once the benchmark data set has been selected, analytical procedures (frequency and time series analyses) are performed to determine whether the subsets of concern are the same or different from the benchmark.

What Is a Benchmark Data Set?

The use of a benchmark data set is based on the premise that the conditions in the marketplace (environmental, economical, geographical, competitive, etc.) act in a similar manner across all business entities that compete in that market segment. Provided there are no conditions to the contrary, these market conditions should continue to act on the various business entities in a similar manner. From a data analysis perspective, this means that similar trends should be apparent in data collected from different sources (such as different business entities, different time periods, etc.), provided that the data relates to the same market segment.

Conditions to the contrary refer to unusual events that disrupt business processes and the effective operations of the business entity or organizational unit. Such conditions could include accounting, organizational, environmental, and technological changes that are large enough to impact the successful operations of the business entity. It is critical that the auditor become familiar with the relevant market environment and identify conditions that might have caused abnormal changes in the business entity that might subsequently be reflected in the data analysis. This is so they are not confused with other patterns in the data identified from the current risk assessment.

Given that the auditor is now juggling two data sets, for clarification, the data set that is the focus of the audit will be called the *data set of concern* and the comparison data set will be called the *benchmark data set*.

If data from different sources is impacted in a similar manner within the same market segment, it stands to reason that the application of various analytical procedures should demonstrate similar results in the data set of concern and in the benchmark data set. If data is impacted by other extraneous variables (particularly those associated with the data of concern), the data should behave differently and the difference should be apparent in the analytical procedures.

If a subset in the data set of concern has been identified as high risk, the assumption is that it is different in some way from other subsets and that difference is driven by the nature of it being high risk. Therefore, comparison to similar data from an independent source (benchmark data set) should result in the data of concern (from the high-risk subset) being different in some way. If the data is the same or similar, the auditor concludes that the data cannot be high risk since it reflects what one would expect to see in the marketplace.

Note that the designation of a data subset being high risk does not mean, at this point in the audit cycle, that the auditor knows which controls were compromised or whether noncompliance was a factor. The auditor only knows that the data is not behaving as expected and that the subdivision was driven by risk.

Characteristics of a Benchmark Data Set

Not all benchmark data sets are considered equal. After becoming familiar with the data set of concern, the auditor should begin the process of selecting one or more suitable data sets to be used as benchmarks. The following criteria can be used to evaluate potential benchmark data sets.

Proximity. Is the benchmark data set stored in the same repository as the data set of concern? Being physically close to the data set of concern potentially opens the door to the benchmark data being compromised. This is one of the disadvantages of using prior period data as a benchmark.

Recency. How close in time is the benchmark data set to the data set of concern? More recent periods are preferred because they will more closely reflect current market conditions in the data.

Similarity. How similar is the benchmark data to the data set of concern? The more similar the data, the more closely the subdivisions will match the data set of concern subdivisions.

Note that the three criteria play off each other. Selecting a data set from a different business entity solves the problem of proximity and potentially raises the problem of similarity. If the benchmark data set is too far in the past, market conditions may have changed and would interfere with the identification of abnormalities in the data as a result of high risk. Auditors must be able to defend that the data from their selected benchmark can be viewed as being representative of similar market conditions and low risk. In other words, the data has not been influenced by the same risk factors that have influenced the data set of concern.

Possible Benchmark Data Sets

The question facing the auditor is how to select an appropriate benchmark data set. To simplify the possibilities, note that it is a benchmark *data set*. As mentioned in the previous chapter, data sets are characterized by a series of columns and a large number of rows. Ratios, standards, and industry best practices are not data sets. Typically they are single numbers (expressed as ratios, frequencies, or percentages) and are commonly used to subdivide data sets. They are important and should not be overlooked, but they do not constitute a data set and therefore cannot be used as a benchmark data set.

The auditor must be able to rely on the fact that the chosen data set is low risk. In other words, the data set cannot contain transactions that have been subjected to the same risk factors (such as control evasion, inappropriate or missing controls, fraud, etc.) that the risk assessment has identified as potentially being present in the data set of concern. If the auditor does not have sufficient information about the benchmark data set, there is a possibility that the benchmark data set could be high risk and therefore not a viable comparison for the data set of concern.

Perhaps the most commonly used benchmark data set is a prior period such as the previous year. This is, of course, only appropriate if the audit team has subjected the previous year's data to some form of audit procedures such as a financial statement review or a review of appropriate controls and compliance. Prior year data has the significant advantages of similarity to the data set of concern and recency and the disadvantage of proximity.

Other organizational units or business entities that are not within scope of the current audit also provide potential benchmarks. In these instances, data from the same period as being examined in the current audit can be used as the benchmark data set. Organizational units within the same business entity in which the audit is taking place have a similar trade-off between similarity and proximity as prior period data. However, the relative distance from the organizational unit under study is a positive factor in the selection as a benchmark. As one moves outside the business entity of concern and considers competing business entities, the proximity concern diminishes while similarity of the data (as in the ability to subdivide the data in similar ways) may become a concern.

The internet is a considerable source of data, whether from competing business entities or from professional organizations that collect data from various companies. Simply Googling a list of professional organizations will provide a starting point in a variety of industries such as retail, health care, real estate, manufacturing, etc. Most professional organizations collect data from their members to examine overall trends in their shared marketplace. These trends are typically composed of collapsed data from member businesses and as such are fairly smooth, but they still demonstrate seasonality and what is happening in the marketplace. There are websites such as datausa. io that provide a starting point to search for relevant data from a variety of industries.

How does one know whether the source of the benchmark data participates in the same market segment? Consider various customer characteristics such as age, gender, location, and interests. Consider the nature of the service being provided and what sort of customers would be in the market for that service. It is possible that apparently unrelated businesses may be drawing on the same customer base.

Many auditors consider that financial information would be the preferred data to use as a benchmark. Though auditors seem to be more comfortable with financial data, nonfinancial data is also affected by changes in market conditions. The simplest way to determine possible sources of nonfinancial data is to ask what generates the financial data. A review of the business entity's process flowcharts will list a variety of inputs, varying from raw materials used in manufacturing to a client's investment portfolios. It could include the number of items sold, whether clothing, cars, or buildings, or the number of employees, hours worked, or number of claims processed. Market conditions will affect many different aspects of a business entity's position in the market segment, and much of this data will demonstrate market trends.

Case Study

The Oklahoma State P-Card data provides an opportunity to look at various potential benchmark data sets. It is important to recognize that the data considered as a benchmark should have been subjected to the same market conditions as the data set under concern. Selecting an appropriate benchmark data set begins with examining its demographic characteristics to see if it is similar or different from the data set of concern. In the following example, prior year is compared to current year (year of concern) and various institutions are compared with respect to size and frequency of transactions.

Internal Benchmark—Prior Year

The first most obvious choice for a benchmark would be prior year data. Begin by assuming that the prior year data would be a suitable low-risk benchmark data set. A comparison of the two data sets yields the following information (see **table 3-1**).

Table 3-1: State of Oklahoma, Comparison of 2011–2012 to 2012–2013 Data Sets		
	Benchmark Data Set 2011–2012	**Data of Concern 2012–2013**
Total Number of Transactions	442,184	441,781
Year Month	July 2011 to June 2012	July 2012 to June 2013
Agency Number	111 unique codes	116 unique codes
Agency Name	117 unique codes	121 unique names
Cardholder Last Name	Contains numeric codes (2200 to 87500) and text (last names); a total of 3490 entries.	Contains numeric codes (1000 to 88000) and text (last names); a total of 3505 entries.
Cardholder First Name	Contains text data and numeric data. Those with single digit numeric values are associated with the cardholder's last name that also contains numeric data. The remaining data contains the first initial of the first name.	Contains text data and numeric data. Those with single digit numeric values are associated with the cardholder's last name that also contains numeric data. The remaining data contains the first initial of the first name.
Description	This column contains numeric data, text data, and alphanumeric data. There are 93,468 different descriptions. There are 44 blanks.	This column contains numeric data, text data, and alphanumeric data. There are 87,823 different descriptions.
Amount	This column contains numeric data (dollar format) with both negative (credits) and positive values (expenditures). The highest dollar value is $1, 157,092.14 and the lowest dollar value (the largest credit) is $78,289.12.	This column contains numeric data (dollar format) with both negative (credits) and positive values (expenditures). The highest dollar value is $1, 764,140.27 and the lowest dollar value (the largest credit) is $99,999.99.
Vendor	This column contains text data, numeric data, and alphanumeric data. There are 92,375 different vendor names/codes.	This column contains text data, numeric data, and alphanumeric data. There are 90,728 different vendor names/codes.
Transaction Date and Posting Date	The transaction date and posting date did not need to be reconfigured.	The transaction date was reconfigured to allow for time series analysis. The post date was not reconfigured.
Merchant Category Code (MCC)	This column contains text data. There are 519 different codes, including blanks.	This column contains text data. There are 496 different codes, including blanks.

In terms of quantity and similarity of data in the columns, the benchmark data set (2011–2012) mirrors the data set of concern (2012–2013) very well.

Now, consider the data for the various agencies, particularly for the 12 largest agencies. *One of the challenges of using historical data is that things change over time.* In this case, the Oklahoma Department of Central Services (DCS) was dissolved in 2011. DCS was responsible for providing services to help manage and support the basic functioning of all state agencies by providing government-wide purchasing, supplying, operation, and maintenance of state property, buildings, and equipment, and for the sale of surplus items. DCS also managed the state motor vehicle fleet and provided government-wide risk management, printing and distribution, and strategic financial and administrative support. DCS was consolidated into the Office of State Finance in 2011. Later in 2012, the agency was renamed to the Oklahoma Office of Management and Enterprise Services (OMES). OMES provides financial, property, purchasing, human resources, and information technology services to all state agencies.

As was mentioned previously, the internet is another best friend of the auditor. There is a wealth of information on the internet, including some very relevant historical information such as name changes in government departments.

Table 3-2 compares the 2011–2012 total frequency of P-Card transactions with the 2012–2013 total frequencies for the top 12 agencies.

Table 3-2: State of Oklahoma 2011–2012 vs 2012–2013, Agency and Total Frequency		
Agency Name	**Frequency 2011–2012**	**Frequency 2012–2013**
Oklahoma State University	123,526	116,179
University of Oklahoma	94,468	81,711
University of Oklahoma Health Sciences Center	60,813	57,942
Department of Corrections	19,716	22,394
Department of Transportation	14,253	15,756
Department of Tourism and Recreation	13,103	15,724
Grand River Dam Authority	8,831	9,749
Department of Rehabilitation Services	8,707	8,628
Southwestern Oklahoma State University	7,636	7,538
Department of Veterans Affairs	6,385	7,483
Office of Management and Enterprise Services*	5,441	7,038
Mental Health and Substance Abuse Services	5,355	5,959

*Note that in 2011, this department was called the Department of Central Services, later named the Office of State Finance and then the Office of Management and Enterprise Services.

Note that there is not a lot of variation from year to year, particularly in the larger agencies. Some frequencies went up, likely indicating a growth year, while others went down. It is of interest to note that the total number of transactions went down from 2011–2012 to 2012–2013 for the four educational institutions listed in the table. Similar trends are apparent in the total dollar amount, as can be seen in **table 3-3**.

Agency Name	Total Dollar Amount 2011–2012	Total Dollar Amount 2012–2013
Table 3-3: State of Oklahoma 2011–2012 vs 2012–2013, Agency and Total Dollar Amount		
Oklahoma State University	$48,761,937.16	$35,211,579.45
University of Oklahoma	$42,284,141.45	$30,527,905.31
University of Oklahoma Health Sciences Center	$23,711,064.09	$22,603,378.77
Grand River Dam Authority	$20,011,163.91	$17,640,224.57
Department of Corrections	$12,032,745.85	$14,284,326.11
Department of Transportation	$9,696,869.53	$11,570,911.87
Department of Tourism and Recreation	$4,303,926.15	$5,277,328.81
Department of Veterans Affairs	$3,303,678.43	$3,779,556.79
Office of Management and Enterprise Services*	$2,726,052	$3,612,959.16
Oklahoma Military Department	$2,813,117.51	$3,363,247.3
Department of Rehabilitation Services	$2,773,790.24	$2,624,413.99
State Department of Health	$3,358,958.58	$2,359,363.73

*Note that in 2011, this department was called the Department of Central Services, later named the Office of State Finance and then the Office of Management and Enterprise Services.

Though further analysis will confirm this finding, at this point 2011–2012 appears to be a viable benchmark to compare with 2012–2013 from the standpoint of number of transactions, total dollar amount, and relative positioning with other agencies, particularly as it relates to those agencies with the most transactions.

External Benchmark—Oklahoma State University

At this point in the analysis, assume that the University of Oklahoma is the focus of the audit. Founded in 1890, the University of Oklahoma is a public research university located in Norman, Oklahoma. In the fall of 2012, which is the period under study, the student enrollment was 31,097, up from 30,753 in the prior year.

As can be seen from the previous discussion, the prior year for the University of Oklahoma would be a viable benchmark for the 2012–2013 data. Another potential benchmark would be a similar business entity—in this case, Oklahoma State University. Oklahoma State University is a public research university located in Stillwater,

Oklahoma, and was also founded in 1890. It is the flagship institution of the Oklahoma State University System. In the fall of 2012, the student enrollment was 25,544, up from 24, 231 in the fall of 2011.

Table 3-4 lists the 2012–2013 and the 2011–2012 total frequency and total dollar amount for all of the educational institutions in the State of Oklahoma.

Table 3-4: State of Oklahoma, Frequency and Dollar Amount of P-Card Transactions for Educational Institutions 2011–2012 vs 2012–2013				
Educational Institutions	Total Frequency 2011–2012	Total Dollar Amount 2011–2012	Total Frequency 2012–2013	Total Dollar Amount 2012–2013
Oklahoma State University	123,526	$48,761,937.16	116,179	$35,211,579.45
University of Oklahoma	94,468	$42,284,141.45	81,711	$30,527,905.31
University of Oklahoma Health Sciences Center	60,813	$23,711,064.09	57,942	$22,603,378.77
Southwestern Oklahoma State University	7,636	$1,336,580.72	7,538	$1,414,258.76
Oklahoma Panhandle State University	4,215	$757,131.64	4,486	$734,321.94
Tulsa Community College	2,689	$2,536,376.69	4,389	$2,055,347.84
Oklahoma Department of Career and Technology Education	2,452	$1,154,438.28	3,739	$1,682,948.83
Redlands Community College	3,696	$1,558,518.59	2,329	$737,378.89
Langston University	1,623	$344,963.35	1,654	$445,964.42
Eastern Oklahoma State College	904	$219,857.71	1,344	$325,048.2
Oklahoma City Community College	636	$246,561.97	802	$349,226.26
Rose State College	522	$142,612.65	695	$219,007.67
Northeastern Oklahoma A&M College	119	$32,884.01	503	$103,592.53
University of Science and Arts of Oklahoma	530	$159,108.03	459	$135,567.07
Oklahoma School of Science & Mathematics	243	$95,275.35	217	$104,468.92
Regional University System of Oklahoma	177	$33,426.44	207	$43,623.34
TOTAL	304,249	$123,374,878.1	284,194	$96,693,618.2

It is interesting to note that the institution with the third largest number of total frequency of P-Card expenditures and total dollar amount is the University of Oklahoma Health Sciences Center, which is the health sciences branch of the University of Oklahoma. Located in Oklahoma City, it serves as the primary place of instruction for many of Oklahoma's health professionals. In the fall of 2012, it had a student enrollment of 3,605, which was down slightly from the 3,625 enrolled in the fall of 2011. The Health Sciences Center has seven patient care institutions associated with it and a variety of educational and research institutions. The Health Sciences Center is the core of a wider complex known as the Oklahoma Health Center. The major clinical facilities on campus are part of the University of Oklahoma College of Medicine and include the University of Oklahoma

Medical Center hospital complex, The Children's Hospital, University of Oklahoma Physicians and University of Oklahoma Children's Physicians clinics, Harold Hamm Diabetes Center, and the Peggy and Charles Stephenson Oklahoma Cancer Center. The large number of institutions and services will in part account for why the number of P-Card expenditures and total dollar amounts is so high compared to a relatively small student enrollment of just over 3,600.

Table 3-5 compares the three educational institutions as a proportion of the total for all educational institutions with respect to total frequency of P-Card transactions and total dollar amount.

Table 3-5: Oklahoma State University, University of Oklahoma, and University of Oklahoma Health Sciences Center 2011–2012 vs 2012–2013 Total Frequency and Total Dollar Amount				
	Total Frequency of Transactions		Total Dollar Amount	
	2011–2012	2012–2013	2011–2012	2012–2013
Oklahoma State University	41%	41%	40%	36%
University of Oklahoma	31%	29%	34%	32%
University of Oklahoma Health Sciences Center	20%	20%	19%	23%
TOTAL	92%	90%	93%	91%

It can be seen that the three institutions together account for more than 90% of the total number of P-Card transactions and total dollar amount for all of the state educational institutions in the State of Oklahoma. The trends in **table 3-5** are roughly similar; however, that finding will be verified with the analytical procedures. What is apparent at this point in the analysis is that Oklahoma State University would be a viable benchmark to look at the remaining two institutions.

In addition to the relative number of transactions and total dollar value of P-Card transactions, the auditor must also be satisfied that the Oklahoma State University data represents a state of low risk. If this was an internal organizational unit, the auditor could rely on past audits as evidence of the state of low risk. For an external business entity, it comes down to ensuring that the business entity is subject to the same market conditions. In this case, the institutions have similar characteristics—they are in the same state and are both public universities that offer a wide variety of programs at different levels with student enrollments roughly the same for Oklahoma State University and the University of Oklahoma. Secondly, there must be assurance that nothing has transpired in the business environment that would lend suspicion to Oklahoma State University either being influenced by the same risk factors as the University of Oklahoma or being subjected to different risk factors to such an extent that the characterization of low risk would be questioned.

The auditor should always consider other potential benchmarks. At a high level, P-Card expenditures can be viewed as a rough measure of work. Work by staff in a university setting is, for the most part, driven by the number of students, number of classes, number of teaching staff, and the quantity and nature of the research performed at the institution. Hours worked by staff, either teaching or performing research, the number of published research papers, the dollar values of grants, etc. could be viable benchmarks. There are many possible sources of benchmark data available, the only requirement being the creativity and curiosity of the auditor.

Summary – What's Important

- Benchmark data sets are data sets with rows and columns. They are not ratios, standards, or industry best practices—which should be used to subdivide data sets.

- Always consider the proximity, recency, and similarity of the benchmark data set to the data set of concern when evaluating its usefulness as a benchmark.

- Possible benchmark data sets include:

  - ☐ Prior year
  - ☐ Other organizational units
  - ☐ Other business entities
  - ☐ Nonfinancial data within the same or different business entity

- The benchmark data must be subject to the same market conditions as the data set of concern.

- The auditor must be able to defend the benchmark data set as being subject to the same market conditions and being low risk.

Case Study

- Note the comparisons used in the case study to determine whether prior year and Oklahoma State University would be suitable benchmarks.

Chapter 4

FREQUENCY ANALYSIS

Frequency analysis is an analytical procedure that uses frequency distributions to compare two columns of numerical data. One column of data comes from the data set of concern and the second from the benchmark data set. Both data sets have already been subjected to subdivision using information garnered from the risk assessment.

The purpose of the frequency analysis is to answer the question, "Is the subset of data from the data set of concern the same as the corresponding subset from the benchmark data set?" If the two subsets are deemed to be similar, then, since the benchmark data set is considered low risk, the subset from the data set of concern must also be low risk. If the two subsets are considered to be different, then the difference is assumed to be driven by risk (since the subdivision was based on risk) and the subset from the data set of concern is considered to be high risk. The analytical tools used to determine the same or different decision are the frequency distribution (in either graphical or tabular format) and measures of central tendency (mean, median, and mode).

What Is a Frequency Distribution?

A frequency distribution is a distribution displayed on a two-axis graph in which the vertical axis represents total frequency and the horizontal axis represents value (typically dollar value). Though a computer will perform calculations and graph data, it typically does so by using all of the individual data points. From a graphical perspective, this results in a great deal of noise or jaggedness in the curve.

Grouping the data into equal intervals alleviates the problem somewhat so that the curve becomes smoother and the shape of the curve can be determined. However, if the number of intervals is too small (i.e., less than five), the shape of the distribution is lost. With practice, the auditor will gain a feeling for the data and choose an appropriate interval width that does not result in too few or too many intervals. Note that the interval width must be equal, particularly at the ends of the distribution.

Different Shapes of Curves

Before delving into frequency analysis, it would be worthwhile to review some of the more commonly found shapes in frequency distributions.

Uniform Distribution

A uniform distribution is a line graph that is parallel to the horizontal axis. In other words, it depicts a situation in which a range of values have the same frequency (see **figure 4-1**).

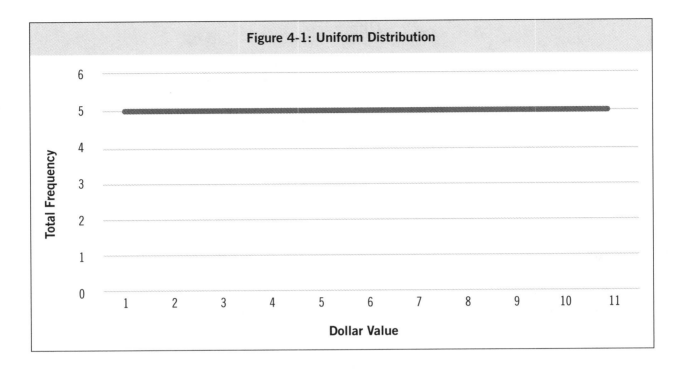

This shape is highly unusual and seldom found in the business environment. If it is discovered, it should be noted and treated as an unusual or unexpected occurrence.

Skewed Distribution

The skewed distribution is an asymmetrical curve with a hump that is off center and one tail that is much longer than the other. Because the skewed distribution can have two different shapes (mirror images of each other), the naming convention is dependent on the location of the tail (see **figure 4-2**).

Of particular interest to auditors is the curve that is skewed to the right. This curve typically reflects the shape of financial data. It is unfortunate that many auditors have never graphed financial data and often assume that it is normal in shape, which in turn leads to the improper use of mean to describe the central tendency of financial data. The hump of the skewed to the right curve represents the relatively larger number of low-dollar value transactions. The long tail to the right represents the much fewer high-dollar transactions that are often referred to as the *outliers*.

Bimodal Distribution

The bimodal curve can be symmetrical or asymmetrical and is distinguished by the presence of two humps in the distribution (see **figure 4-3**). The humps do not necessarily have to be equal in size. The presence of two humps means that there are likely two different distributions of data combined into a single subset. The challenge facing the auditor is how to separate the data into its components.

It is possible that the bimodal distribution actually looks like the following two distributions combined (see **figure 4-4**). If the distribution were simply cut in half, this would result in a mix of the two distributions within each half.

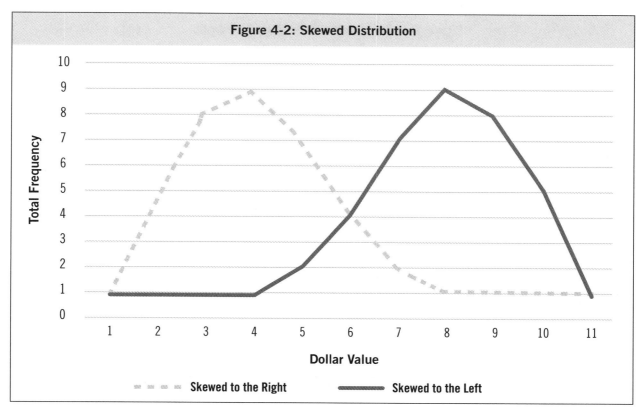

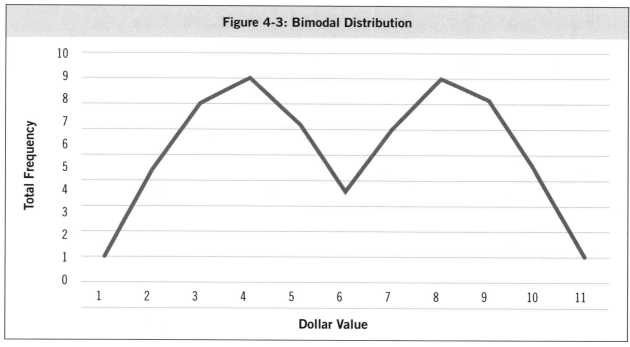

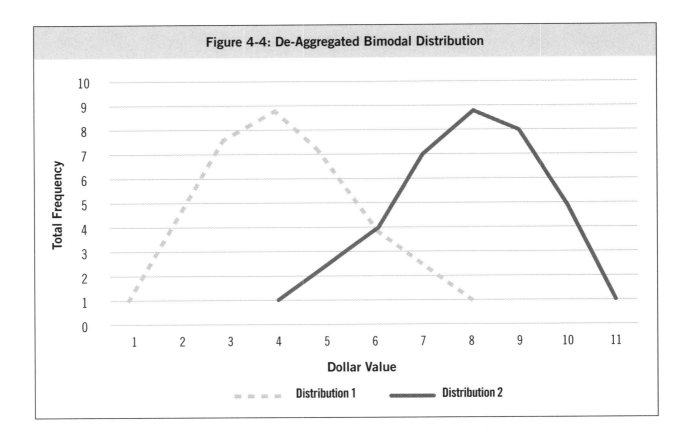

Figure 4-4: De-Aggregated Bimodal Distribution

Separating the bimodal distribution into its component distributions requires the auditor to continue to subdivide the subset to a lower level of aggregation. Subsets such as data at a facility level can be further subdivided down to the shift level, or regional aggregates can be subdivided to cities or facilities.

Normal Distribution

The normal distribution is the most well-known distribution, which has not always worked to its advantage. It is often assumed that most data (if not all data) will display a normal distribution when graphed. The reality is that organically driven data such as human performance (physical, psychological, educational) and data collected from the earth's plants and animals will display a normal distribution. Data that is driven by industry, particularly by dollar value, displays a skewed distribution. Process metrics, which include metrics that measure human performance, will be normally distributed, while those metrics that measure financial or quality performance will be skewed. The normal distribution is a symmetrical single hump curve with tails that are relatively the same length (see **figure 4-5**).

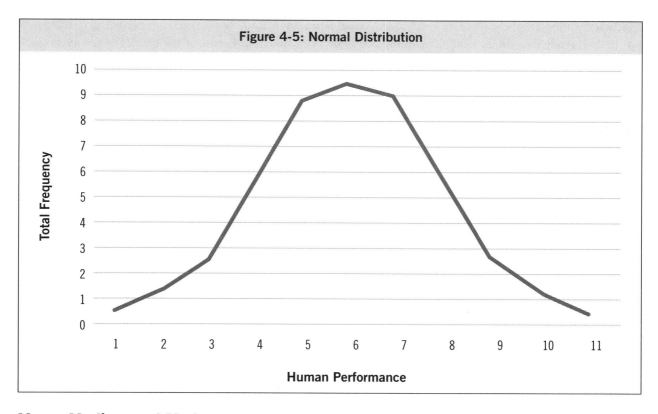

Figure 4-5: Normal Distribution

Mean, Median, and Mode

The mean, median, and mode are the three measures of central tendency, which is defined as the place in the frequency distribution where the majority of the transactions/scores are located. They have a very specific relationship when it comes to skewed distributions, and that relationship is leveraged in frequency analysis.

Mean (or average) is the most well-known measure of central tendency. In fact, it is so well-known that it is frequently misused. The mean has two assumptions. The first deals with the nature of the variable being tabulated. The variable must be continuous or, in other words, if divided using arithmetic division, the result must exist in reality. Consider the popular metric, "the average number of children in a household." Typically it is something like 3.2 or 3.5 children per household. Have you ever seen .5 of a child? Of course not, yet this metric is frequently cited even though it does not meet the first assumption of the mean. The second assumption is that the mean, as a measure of central tendency, can only be calculated on normally distributed data. In other words, calculating a mean based on skewed data (such as financial data) misrepresents the central tendency. This will be seen later when the relationship among the mean, median, and mode is discussed. The mean is the most sophisticated measure of central tendency and is dependent on both the value and frequency of the transactions/scores. Consequently, the location of the mean is greatly influenced by the outliers or length of the tail of the frequency distribution, particularly if the distribution is skewed. As such, the mean is an indication of the tail in a skewed distribution.

Median is the 50% cut point when the transactions/scores are rank ordered. When the number of transactions/scores is odd, the median is the middle score. When the number of scores is even, the median is located halfway between the two middle scores. The median is more sophisticated than the mode because it relies on the frequency of all transactions/scores. Visually the median (50% cut point) divides the area under the frequency distribution into two equal halves. As such, the median provides an indicator of the location of the hump in the frequency distribution, particularly when the distribution is skewed.

Mode is the most frequent score. It is the most unsophisticated measure of central tendency because it depends on the frequency of a single score. The mode is not always a strong indicator of the central tendency because the single most frequent score could lie anywhere in the hump. Within a frequency distribution, the mode is considered to be the peak.

Relationships Among the Mean, Median, and Mode

In a normal distribution, the mean, median, and mode have the same value. This is a result of the frequency distribution being a single hump symmetrical distribution (see **figure 4-6**).

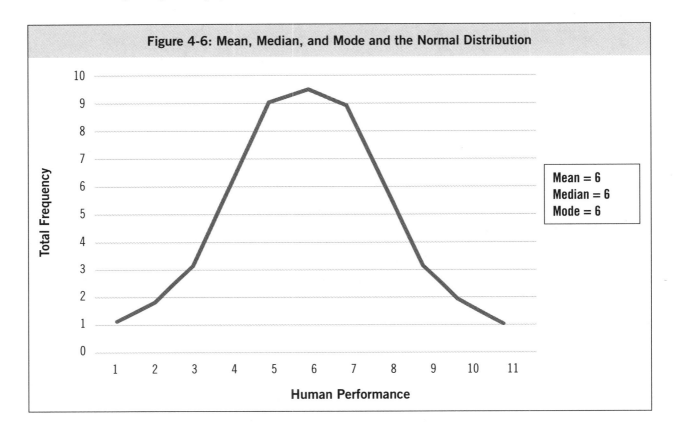

Figure 4-6: Mean, Median, and Mode and the Normal Distribution

In a skewed distribution, the relationship is quite different. As can be seen in **figure 4-7**, the measures of central tendency are spread out rather than clustered together.

In this distribution, the mode is slightly less than the median. This is not always the case. The position of the mode could be anywhere in the hump of the distribution, either above or below the median. The median is always somewhere in the hump of the distribution. The position of the mean varies depending on the length of the tail and the frequencies of the scores in the tail. When the tail is long, the mean is pulled toward the few high-dollar transactions. With shorter tails, the mean lies closer to the center of the distribution's hump.

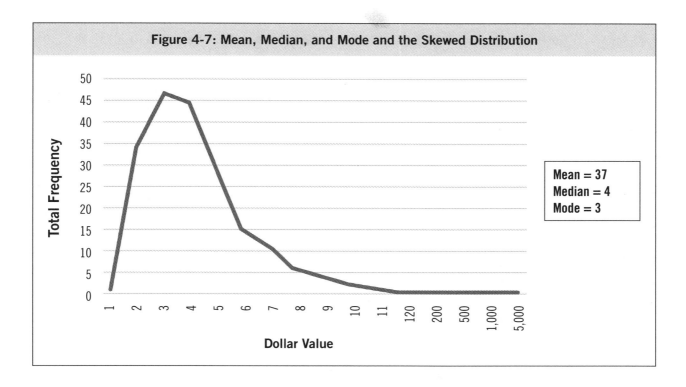

Figure 4-7: Mean, Median, and Mode and the Skewed Distribution

Mean = 37
Median = 4
Mode = 3

The distance between the three measures of central tendency is often used as an ad hoc measure of skewness. When the three measures of central tendency are close together, the distribution approaches a normal distribution. When the three central tendencies lie very far apart, the distribution is considered to be skewed.

Differentiating Between the Data Set of Concern and the Benchmark Data Set

The benchmark data set was selected as a suitable comparison because it was deemed to be low risk. If the data set of concern is also low risk, then when the two sets of data are graphed, the curves should be very similar. When the measures of central tendency are calculated, there should be little difference between those calculated from the benchmark data and those from the data of concern. When there is a difference, the difference is assumed to be driven by risk because the subdivision of the data set was based on risk.

Figure 4-8 demonstrates what is meant by little difference between the two distributions. Note that the measures of central tendency are also very close to each other when the mode of the benchmark data is compared to the mode of the data of concern, the median to the median and the mean to the mean.

The next two curves demonstrate potential differences in shape of the curves. It is important to identify where the curves diverge from each other. In other words, where the data of concern diverges from what is expected (the shape of the benchmark data). In the first instance (see **figure 4-9**), the hump has grown in size and has shifted to the right. Because the tails remain the same length, the increase in the size of the hump serves to pull the mean toward it. Note that while the mean has shifted to the left, the mode and median have shifted to the right. The movement of the mean to the left is a function of the higher frequency of scores in the beginning part of the tail.

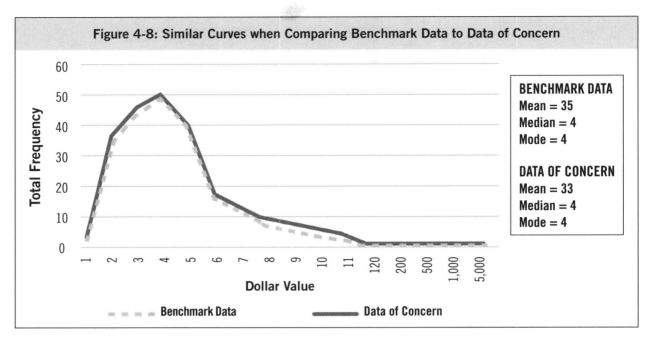

Figure 4-8: Similar Curves when Comparing Benchmark Data to Data of Concern

BENCHMARK DATA
Mean = 35
Median = 4
Mode = 4

DATA OF CONCERN
Mean = 33
Median = 4
Mode = 4

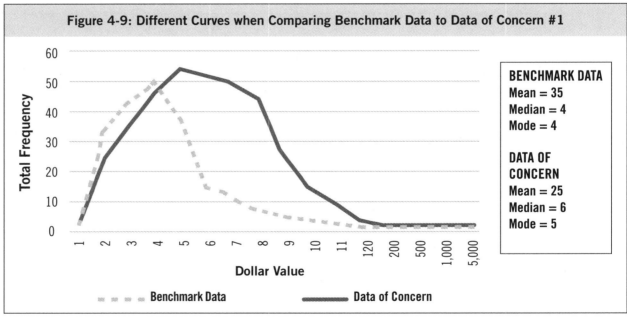

Figure 4-9: Different Curves when Comparing Benchmark Data to Data of Concern #1

BENCHMARK DATA
Mean = 35
Median = 4
Mode = 4

DATA OF CONCERN
Mean = 25
Median = 6
Mode = 5

The next curve demonstrates two curves with different tails (see **figure 4-10**). Note that the hump in the tail pulls the median slightly toward it and has a much greater effect on the mean.

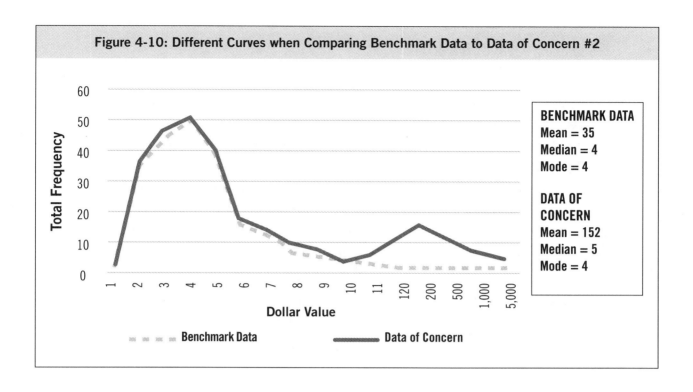

Figure 4-10: Different Curves when Comparing Benchmark Data to Data of Concern #2

BENCHMARK DATA
Mean = 35
Median = 4
Mode = 4

DATA OF CONCERN
Mean = 152
Median = 5
Mode = 4

Why Use a Frequency Distribution and Central Tendency?

In many cases, the benchmark data will have the same units of measurement as the data of concern. This will obviously be true when prior year data is used. Selecting whether to use a graphical technique first or calculate measures of central tendency first comes down to a matter of personal preference. The advantage of calculating the measures of central tendency is that differences in the shape that are not apparent in the graph will become apparent when the various measures of central tendency are calculated. The central tendencies have a further advantage of pointing the auditor to which portion of the data (peak, hump, or tail) the differences are located. For displaying differences to an audience—either management, clients, audit management, or audit committee— a graphical presentation is always preferred.

The units of measurement will change from the benchmark to the data of concern if nonfinancial data is compared to financial data. In this instance, assessing similarities in shape of a distribution provides more information than the measures of central tendency.

Summary – What's Important

- Frequency analysis uses the shape of the frequency distribution and the measures of central tendency to determine whether the two columns of data (one from the benchmark data set and one from the data set of concern) are the same or different.

- Because the subdivision was based on risk and the benchmark was selected based on it being low risk, the following conclusions can be drawn:

  ☐ When there is not a noticeable difference between the benchmark and the data set of concern, the subset from the data set of concern is assumed to be low risk.

  ☐ When there is a noticeable difference between the benchmark and the data set of concern, the difference is assumed to be driven by risk.

- Once a noticeable difference has been found, the difference must be validated with management. If information from management further validates the assumption of high risk, the subset from the data set of concern will be considered as a potential candidate for examination of transactions.

Chapter 5

FREQUENCY ANALYSIS CASE STUDY

Preparing the Data Set for Analysis

The tool that auditors will be using in this analysis is the pivot table. Before using pivot tables, auditors should be familiar with the following functions in Excel.

Activity or Metric	Excel Function	Instructions
Sorting data based on certain columns	Sort	Sort the columns from the data set of concern based on the date column so that the rows are in chronological order. Click on the data tab in the top toolbar of the spreadsheet. Highlight all of the data fields in the subset, including the header row (labels of the columns). To do this, click on a single cell in the data set, then press Ctrl followed by A. Click on the Sort icon. In the dialog box, make sure that 'My data has headers' is checked (upper right corner). Go to 'Sort by' and chose the column being used to sort the data (i.e., date). Make sure that all data fields have been selected (highlighted), otherwise some will be sorted and some will not, effectively mixing up your data set.

Activity or Metric	Excel Function	Instructions
Measures of central tendency—mode, median, and mean	MODE.SNGL, MEDIAN, AVERAGE	Go to Formulas - More functions - Statistical – select MODE.SNGL, MEDIAN, AVERAGE. When the dialogue box comes up, enter the first array, called 'Number 1,' and enter the first cell of your data and the last cell of your data, separated by a colon (e.g., a2:a407). Note that for MODE.SNGL, if an 'NA' appears in the cell, this means that the excel program was unable to find any duplicates. In this case, sort the data by value and use FREQUENCY to create a frequency distribution.

In preparation for pivot tables, there can be no blank cells in the data set. The following instructions deal with placing some text (such as No Response) in the blank cells. Note that in more recent versions of Excel, pivot tables can handle blank cells.

Activity or Metric	Excel Function	Instructions
Replace blank cell with text		One way you can fill in these blank cells is to click once on cell A1 and then press Ctrl A to select the list. Press Ctrl G to display the Go To dialog box and then click the Special button. Double-click on Blanks, which will result in just the blank cells being selected. Type the words No Response and then press Ctrl Enter. Doing so will put the words No Response in all of the selected cells at once.

To prepare for a frequency analysis, frequency intervals will need to be created for the dollar amounts listed in the data set. The frequency intervals allow the data to be graphed so that differences in two sets of data can be assessed. For the Oklahoma data, a variety of frequency intervals were used ranging from $200 up to $10,000. The number of intervals varies depending on what the auditor is examining, which in some cases might be the complete column of dollar amounts, and in other cases only a specific portion of the column.

Activity or Metric	Excel Function	Instructions
Creating intervals for frequency analysis	"=ceiling(A2, 200)"	Sort the dollar value data from lowest to highest.
		Divide the dollar value data into intervals. The number of intervals should not be less than five. The maximum number of intervals will depend on the range covered by the data. The intervals should be of equal size.
		Begin by using an interval width that is suitable for the complete data set. Once you subdivide, readjust the interval width to suit the individual subsets.
		In the first cell of a blank column adjacent to the column containing the dollar value data, type =ceiling(A2, 200). This command says to take the dollar value in cell A2 (assuming that the dollar value data is in column A) and round it up to a value of 200. If the dollar value is greater than 200, it will round up to 400; if greater than 400, it will round up to 600. As can be seen in this example, 200 is the interval width. Copy the formula and then paste it into all of the cells in the column adjacent to the column containing the dollar data so that every cell in the dollar data column has the formula pasted beside it. The easiest way to do this is to create the formula in your toolbar with your cursor in the first cell. Move your cursor to the bottom right corner until a plus sign appears. Double click on the plus sign. The formula will be copied down the column, provided there is data in the column to the left.

Once frequency intervals have been included in the data set, the auditor can begin to form pivot tables.

Activity or Metric	Excel Function	Instructions
Calculating the total frequency within each of the specified frequency intervals	Pivot Tables	Highlight/select all cells you wish to examine in the subset, including column headings. To do this, click on a single cell in the data set and press Ctrl A. If you are doing several pivot tables in the same spreadsheet, separate the rows and cut and paste the column headings for each subdivision. This way it will be easier to identify which columns and rows you wish to select. Click on the Insert tab in the toolbar at the top of the spreadsheet. Select Pivot Table (upper left corner). A dialog box will appear. The selected cells (using the column labels) are pre-populated in the upper portion of the box. In the lower portion, select Existing Worksheet and input a cell (e.g., i25 – with column and row identifier) that is to the right of the columns you are examining where you would like the pivot table to appear on your worksheet. Click Okay. A dialog box will appear to the far right of your screen. If you scroll over to the right, you will see a space marked for the location of the pivot table. In the upper portion of the dialog box (Pivot Table Field List), there is a list of the column headings. Select the dollar value column, the name column, and the interval name column. In the lower portion of the dialog box, the interval name column will appear as a row label. The dollar value appears to the right in the sum box. This will provide a sum for the dollar values within each of the interval names. Drag the Name Column from the upper portion of the dialog box to the sum box. This will provide a frequency count of the number of times the Name appears in each interval. If there is more than one name, the pivot table will subdivide to show separate frequency counts. Another method is to copy the word Count into every cell in a separate column. Using the Count label in the Sum box will provide totals for each subdivision. The pivot table will appear on your spreadsheet as the above actions are performed.

Once a pivot table has been created, graphing the result is simple.

Activity or Metric	Excel Function	Instructions
Graphing a frequency distribution from a pivot table	Insert/graph type	Columns can be highlighted directly from the pivot table and then graphed. Simply highlight the frequency interval column and the columns of frequencies listed in the pivot table into a separate worksheet (excluding totals, but including the column headings for the frequencies; do not include a heading for the frequency intervals or it will appear as a line on the graph). Pair up the data of concern and the benchmark data so that the time intervals align exactly. Highlight the two columns of data, click on Insert, select the appropriate graph, and click on its icon.

Become Familiar with the Market Conditions: State of Oklahoma

It is always a good idea to become familiar with the data and the environment in which it was created. In this instance, looking at the total set of data for the State of Oklahoma provides the context for the university data and an opportunity to fine-tune their expectations for the university data. A review of major events both in the marketplace and with respect to the individual educational institutions should be completed to identify known abnormalities that may already exist in the data.

Considering the State of Oklahoma data for 2012–2013, there are 441,781 transactions. The minimum value is -$99,999.99 and the maximum dollar value is $1,764,140.27. Given this considerable range, a variety of frequency intervals will be needed. Using an interval width of $10,000, **figure 5-1** displays the typical skewed distribution that characterizes financial data.

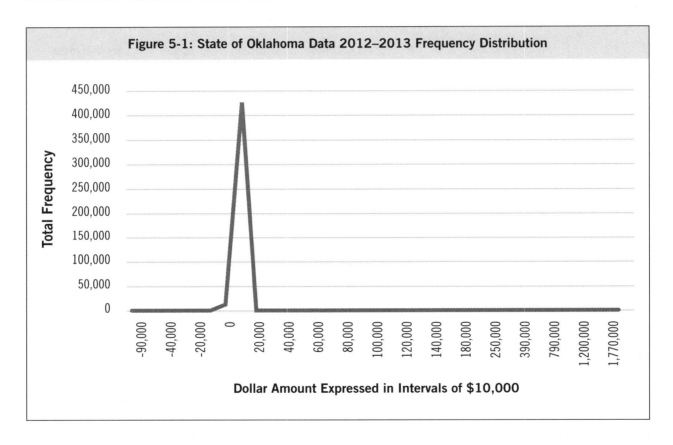

Figure 5-1: State of Oklahoma Data 2012–2013 Frequency Distribution

Reducing the interval width to $5,000 produces similar frequency distribution (see **figure 5-2**). Decreasing the interval width increases the number of intervals (which could be problematic when graphing) but provides a more detailed view of the data.

The skewed distribution is again apparent. According to the latest policies and procedures for the State of Oklahoma P-Card Program, there is a spending limit of $5,000 for most transactions. Support for this limitation is born out when the above data is expressed in a tabular format and it is found that 99.5% of the transactions are $5,000 or less. Note that there is a list of exceptions in the Oklahoma P-Card Program and readers should not assume that the transactions that exceed $5,000 are necessarily problematic.

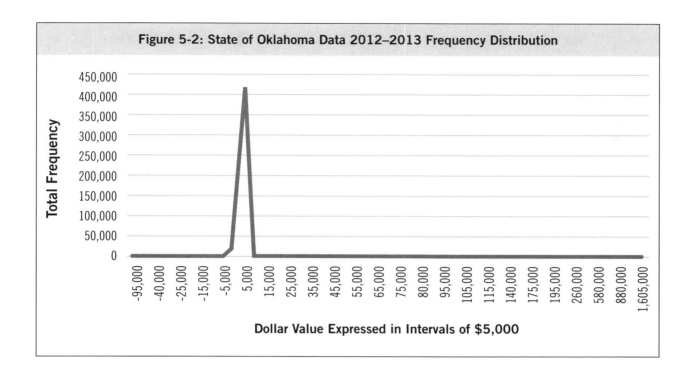

Figure 5-2: State of Oklahoma Data 2012–2013 Frequency Distribution

Validate the Internal Benchmark, Prior Year (2011–2012): State of Oklahoma

Now consider the benchmark data for 2011–2012. There are 442,184 transactions in the data set, with a minimum value of -$78, 289.12 and a maximum value of $1,157,092.14. Of those transactions, 99.2% are equal to or less than $5,000. The first figure displays the data with a frequency interval of $10,000. As can be seen, the humps match very well and the tail for the 2012–2013 is longer than the tail for the 2011–2012 data (see **figure 5-3**).

The data using an interval width of $5,000 illustrates the same pattern as in the $10,000 interval displayed in **figure 5-3**. The difference in the length of the tails is more apparent in **figure 5-4**. In addition, the measures of central tendency are displayed beside the second graph.

Particularly in large data sets, the central tendencies provide some indication of differences between two distributions of frequency data. The mode for both the benchmark and the data of concern is listed as $1,000. Remember that the mode is the single most frequent score and is also the most unsophisticated measure of central tendency. Consequently, though it is frequently (though not always) in the hump, it may not be in the center of the hump. In **table 5-1** (using an interval width of $200), it can be seen that the largest frequency of transactions for both 2011–2012 and 2012–2013 is found in the interval of 0 to $200. The frequency diminishes as the dollar values increase. The corresponding graph (**figure 5-5**) illustrates that the rate of decrease between the two sets of data is almost identical (the 2011–2012 curve matches the 2012–2013 curve so well that only one curve is apparent).

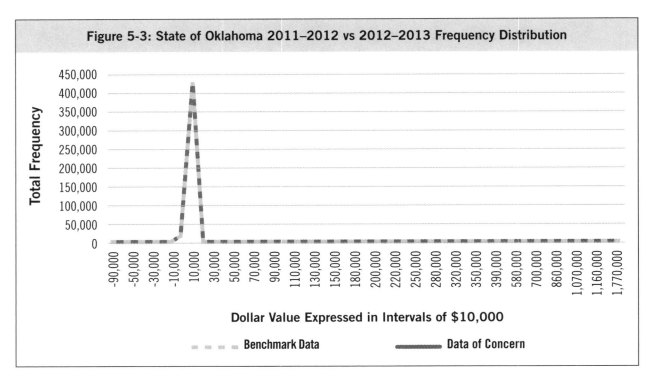

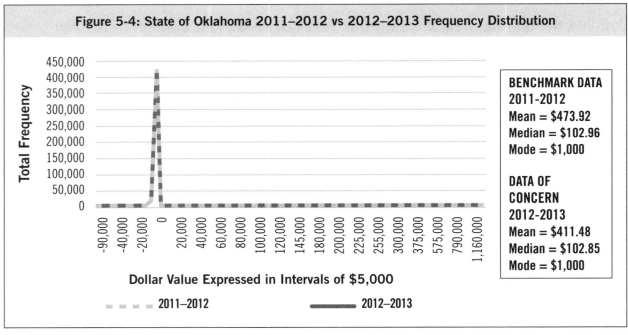

Table 5-1: State of Oklahoma 2011–2012 vs 2012–2013 Frequency Distribution		
Frequency Interval	2011–2012	2012–2013
-$200 to 0	12,108	10,997
0 to $200	268,844	270,230
$200 to $400	61,813	62,328
$400 to $600	33,143	33,177
$600 to $800	16,561	17,024
$800 to $1000	10,043	10,222
$1000 to $1200	6,233	6,108
$1200 to $1400	4,613	4,315

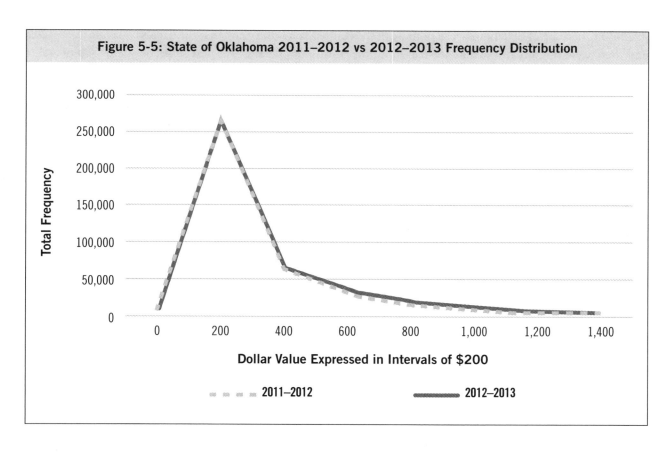

Figure 5-5: State of Oklahoma 2011–2012 vs 2012–2013 Frequency Distribution

The shape of the graph is consistent with the values for the median and the mean. The mode is still a valid measure, but it simply means that the *single most frequent* dollar value is $1,000. Because the mode is to the right of the mean, it may be worthwhile for the auditor to isolate the transactions that are $1,000 simply to see if there is anything unusual occurring.

The purpose behind looking at the total Oklahoma data set is to help the auditors fine-tune their expectations about what would be expected in the university data. This analysis does not take that long and makes a basic use of pivot tables and frequency intervals. It allows the auditors to get a feeling for the shape of the data, particularly the length of the tail. It also may provide more specific information such as the proportion of transactions that exceeds $5,000. The maximum and minimum values provide the full range of the entire data set for comparison to the university data.

Validate the External Benchmark: Oklahoma State University

A total of 58% of the transactions for the Oklahoma State data in 2012–2013 are attributed to Oklahoma State University, the University of Oklahoma, and the University of Oklahoma Health Sciences Center. It stands to reason then that these three institutions should have a similar shape to the Oklahoma State data.

The data is analyzed in exactly the same way as the previous data, with the exception that the data is filtered by agency name so that only the data for the three selected institutions appears. In the first part of the analysis, only the data for Oklahoma State University is considered. It is important to validate the external benchmark. The Oklahoma State University data is compared to the prior year, keeping in mind what was seen in the previous graphs for the State of Oklahoma. The purpose of the comparison is to ensure that the data is behaving as expected and there were not any unusual abnormalities in the prior year's data. In the first series of graphs (**figure 5-6**), a frequency interval of $10,000 is used.

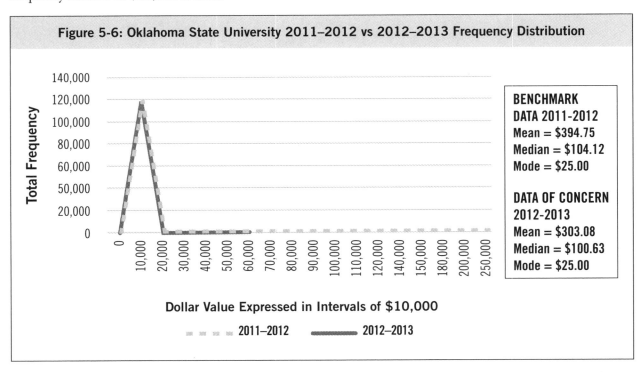

Figure 5-6: Oklahoma State University 2011–2012 vs 2012–2013 Frequency Distribution

The humps match very well, with the prior year being slightly larger. There is a difference in the length of the tails, with the prior year (2011–2012) being much longer than 2012–2013, indicating expenditures above $60,000. The closeness of the humps is reflected in the closeness of the modes and medians to each other in the 2011–2012 and 2012–2013 data. The two means are different, with the higher value in 2011–2012 reflecting the longer tail. This is contrary to the State of Oklahoma data, which has a longer tail in 2012–2013. As will be seen later, this finding does not negate the use of Oklahoma State University as a viable benchmark.

Comparison to the Internal Benchmark: Prior Year (2011–2012)

The frequency analysis begins with the comparison of the University of Oklahoma and the University of Oklahoma Health Sciences Center (data of concern) to their respective prior year data (the internal benchmark). See **figure 5-7**.

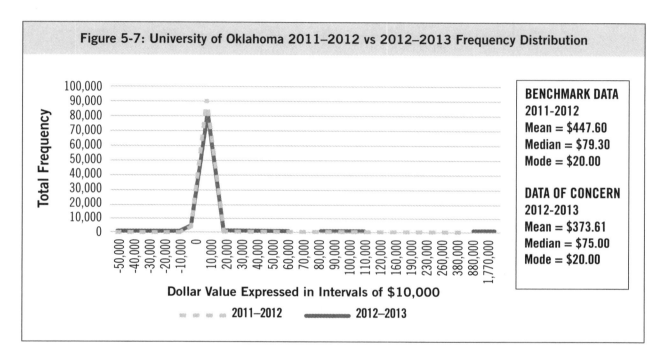

Figure 5-7: University of Oklahoma 2011–2012 vs 2012–2013 Frequency Distribution

BENCHMARK DATA
2011-2012
Mean = $447.60
Median = $79.30
Mode = $20.00

DATA OF CONCERN
2012-2013
Mean = $373.61
Median = $75.00
Mode = $20.00

The University of Oklahoma's data also matches the prior year fairly well. The major differences lie in the tail. Both tails are relatively long, with 2012–2013 being the longest with expenditures exceeding $380,000. The values of the modes and medians support the closeness of the two humps. Note that the means do not line up with the length of the tails. However, remember that the mean is a function of both value and frequency. **Table 5-2** lists the frequencies for University of Oklahoma's 2011–2012 and 2012–2013 data. Note the difference in the tails and pay particular attention to the larger frequencies in the tail of the 2011–2012 data. The larger frequencies in the tail of the 2011–2012 pull the mean more toward the tail than the lower frequencies in the 2012–2013 data.

Table 5-2: University of Oklahoma 2011–2012 vs 2012–2013 Frequency Distribution		
Frequency Interval	2011–2012	2012–2013
-50000	1	
-40000	2	
-30000	2	

Table 5-2: University of Oklahoma 2011–2012 vs 2012–2013 Frequency Distribution (continued)		
-20000	2	3
-10000	5	
0	3,203	2,690
10000	90,747	78,823
20000	292	120
30000	102	32
40000	34	12
50000	36	21
60000	16	3
70000	10	1
80000	3	1
90000	2	
100000	2	1
110000	3	1
120000	1	
160000	1	
190000	1	
230000	1	
260000	1	
380000	1	
880000		1
1610000		1
1770000		1

It is important to understand the interplay of the measures of central tendency with the shape of the frequency distribution. The graphical and the metric components of frequency analysis each provide a different perspective of the data. Using both provides a more complete picture of the comparison of the data of concern with the benchmark data set.

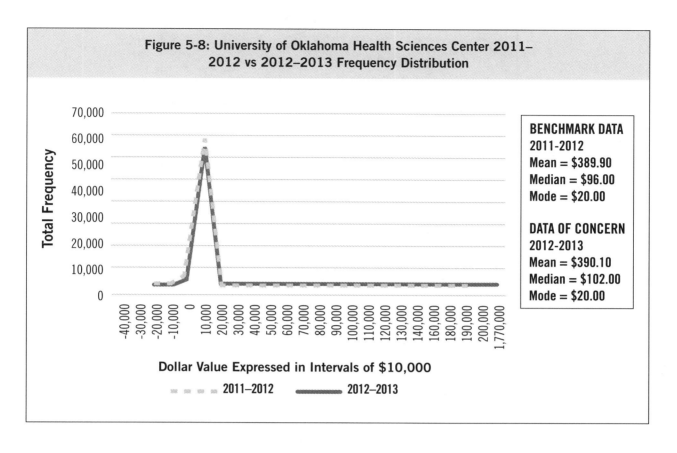

Figure 5-8: University of Oklahoma Health Sciences Center 2011–2012 vs 2012–2013 Frequency Distribution

BENCHMARK DATA
2011-2012
Mean = $389.90
Median = $96.00
Mode = $20.00

DATA OF CONCERN
2012-2013
Mean = $390.10
Median = $102.00
Mode = $20.00

The University of Oklahoma Health Sciences Center's data again matches very well with prior data (see **figure 5-8**). Similar to the previous graphs, there are differences in the length of the tails. The 2012–2013 has expenditures exceeding $190,000. However, the measures of central tendency line up quite closely with each other. **Table 5-3** lists the frequency distributions for both data sets. The tails are different in length, yet the actual frequencies are relatively close to each other. The similar frequencies and the overlapping in the tail between the two distributions result in the means being very close to each other.

Table 5-3: University of Oklahoma Health Sciences Center 2011–2012 vs 2012–2013 Frequency Distribution		
Frequency Interval	2011–2012	2012–2013
-40000		1
-30000	1	
-20000		2
-10000	3	3
0	3,168	2,006
10000	57,434	55,806
20000	121	74

Table 5-3: University of Oklahoma Health Sciences Center 2011–2012 vs 2012–2013 Frequency Distribution (continued)		
Frequency Interval	**2011–2012**	**2012–2013**
30000	32	23
40000	17	4
50000	11	9
60000	3	7
70000	4	
80000	6	2
90000	3	1
100000	2	1
110000		1
120000	1	
130000	1	
140000	3	
160000	1	
180000	1	
190000	1	
200000		1
1770000		1

Once the auditors have reviewed the shape and central tendency of the data of concern and the benchmark data, it is necessary to summarize the findings. Remember that at this stage in the audit process, the concern is not whether controls are failing or whether there is a lack of compliance. Rather, it is about what stands out as being high risk.

What is known thus far. At this point in the analysis, the outliers in the University of Oklahoma and the University of Oklahoma Health Sciences Center remain a concern. For both institutions, the values exceed those found in the prior year. The humps of the data line up quite well with benchmarks so, at this point in the analysis, the humps do not stand out as a concern.

Comparison to the External Benchmark: Oklahoma State University

The next phase of the analysis considers just the 2012–2013 data for the three educational institutions. Oklahoma State University is considered the external benchmark. The comparison with its prior year yielded an interesting difference in the length of the tails, which serves as a reminder that the tails or outliers may change in value from year to year. To balance this perspective is the fact that in 2011–2012, the year where Oklahoma State University has its largest outliers, the maximum value did not exceed $250,000, which is considerably smaller than the outliers in the University of Oklahoma and the University of Oklahoma Health Sciences Center, which exceeded a million dollars.

Figure 5-9 illustrates the comparison of the three institutions for 2012–2013. It is followed by **table 5-4**, which lists the corresponding values for their central tendencies.

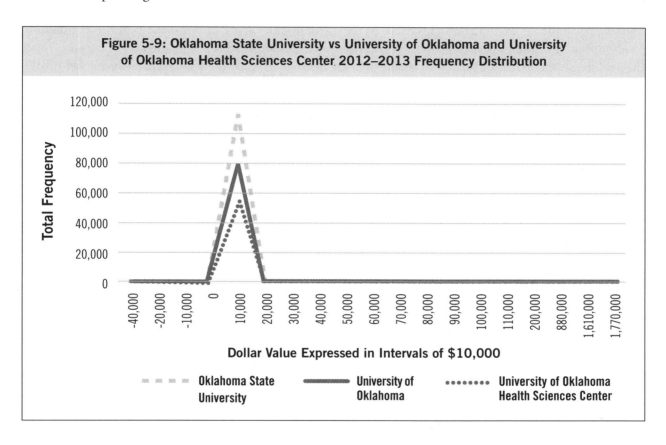

Figure 5-9: Oklahoma State University vs University of Oklahoma and University of Oklahoma Health Sciences Center 2012–2013 Frequency Distribution

Table 5-4: Oklahoma State University, University of Oklahoma, and University of Oklahoma Health Sciences Center 2012–2013 Central Tendency			
	Oklahoma State University	**University of Oklahoma**	**University of Oklahoma Health Sciences Center**
Mean	$303.08	$373.61	$390.10
Median	$100.63	$75.00	$102.00
Mode	$25.00	$20.00	$20.00

The graph and the central tendencies indicate that the hump is relatively compressed and similar between the external benchmark (Oklahoma State University) and the other two institutions. In terms of frequencies, Oklahoma State University has higher frequencies in the hump than the University of Oklahoma or the University of Oklahoma Health Sciences Center. The tails, however, are different, with the University of Oklahoma Health Sciences Center having the largest mean value. At this point in the analysis, it is known that the tails differ from the benchmark, but the exact difference is still unknown. The mean is a reflection of value and frequency, which means the difference could result from frequency, value, or both.

To complete a further examination of the tails of the distributions, the data from the tails of the distributions were graphed. The humps of the distribution are extremely large compared to the frequencies in the tails. To see the pattern in the tails, the frequency for transactions greater than $10,000 is graphed separately (see **figure 5-10**).

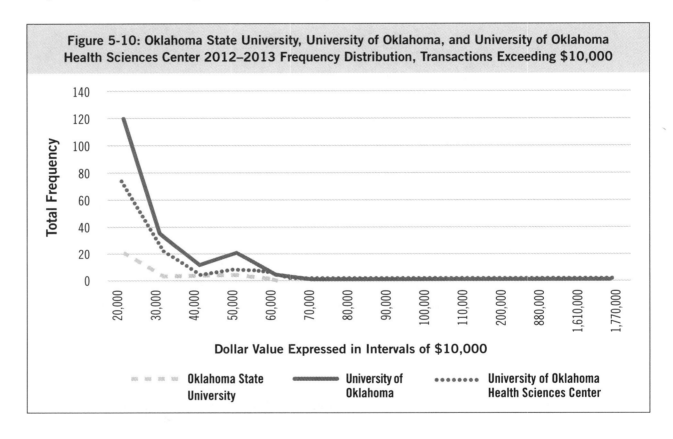

Figure 5-10: Oklahoma State University, University of Oklahoma, and University of Oklahoma Health Sciences Center 2012–2013 Frequency Distribution, Transactions Exceeding $10,000

The graph illustrates that Oklahoma State University, which originally had the highest frequencies in the hump, now has the lowest frequency, whereas the University of Oklahoma demonstrates the highest frequencies in the tails, followed closely by the University of Oklahoma Health Sciences Center. The change in the order of frequencies between the benchmark and the University of Oklahoma institutions is more clearly seen in the tabular format (see **table 5-5**).

	Table 5-5: Oklahoma State University, University of Oklahoma, and University of Oklahoma Health Sciences Center 2012–2013 Frequency Distribution Using a Frequency Interval of $10,000		
Frequency Interval	Oklahoma State University	University of Oklahoma	University of Oklahoma Health Sciences Center
-40000			1
-20000		3	2
-10000			3
0	3,783	2,690	2,006
10000	112,362	78,823	55,806
20000	21	120	74
30000	4	32	23
40000	4	12	4
50000	4	21	9
60000	1	3	7
70000		1	
80000		1	2
90000			1
100000		1	1
110000		1	1
200000			1
880000		1	
1610000		1	
1770000		1	1

First note the relatively small tail for Oklahoma State University. Also note that Oklahoma State University has significantly larger frequencies in the hump than the University of Oklahoma or the University of Oklahoma Health Sciences Center. One would expect that this relationship would continue into the tail of the distribution. Yet the frequencies invert, with the two University of Oklahoma institutions having higher frequencies and longer tails than Oklahoma State University.

Discovering this divergence from what is expected is the objective of data analysis. It remains to be seen whether these transactions are problematic. At this point in the analysis, all that is known is that the frequencies do not follow the expected pattern.

Before going any further in the analysis, a question could be raised as to whether this same pattern occurred in the prior year's data. **Figure 5-11** illustrates the data for 2011–2012, focusing on the tail (i.e., the frequencies of transactions exceeding $10,000).

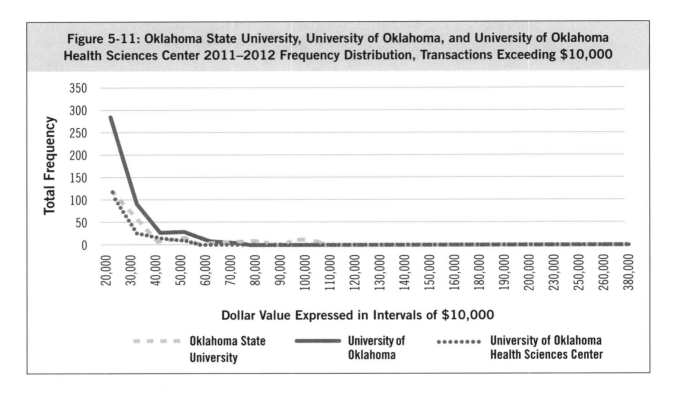

Figure 5-11: Oklahoma State University, University of Oklahoma, and University of Oklahoma Health Sciences Center 2011–2012 Frequency Distribution, Transactions Exceeding $10,000

Several observations are immediately apparent. The interaction seen in the 2012–2013 data is apparent in the prior year's data, but it is not as clearly defined, though University of Oklahoma maintains the position of having the highest frequencies in the tail. The other observation is that the tails are much shorter in the prior year, with no transactions exceeding $380,000. Looking at the data in the tabular format (see **table 5-6**) allows for the comparison of actual frequencies.

Table 5-6: Oklahoma State University, University of Oklahoma, and University of Oklahoma Health Sciences Center 2011–2012 Frequency Distribution			
Frequency Interval	Oklahoma State University	University of Oklahoma	University of Oklahoma Health Sciences Center
-50000		1	
-40000		2	
-30000		2	1
-20000		2	
-10000		5	3
0	4,058	3,203	3,168

Table 5-6: Oklahoma State University, University of Oklahoma, and University of Oklahoma Health Sciences Center 2011–2012 Frequency Distribution (continued)			
Frequency Interval	Oklahoma State University	University of Oklahoma	University of Oklahoma Health Sciences Center
10000	119,216	90,747	57,434
20000	125	292	121
30000	59	102	32
40000	7	34	17
50000	17	36	11
60000	4	16	3
70000	5	10	4
80000	7	3	6
90000	3	2	3
100000	16	2	2
110000	1	3	
120000	2	1	1
130000			1
140000	1		2
150000	2		
160000		1	1
180000	1		1
190000		1	1
200000	1		
230000		1	
250000	1		
260000		1	
380000		1	

Figure 5-12, **figure 5-13**, and **figure 5-14** describe the tails for each educational institution for transactions greater than $10,000.

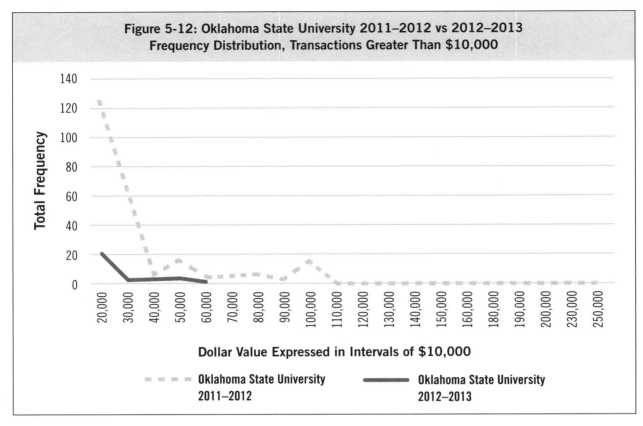

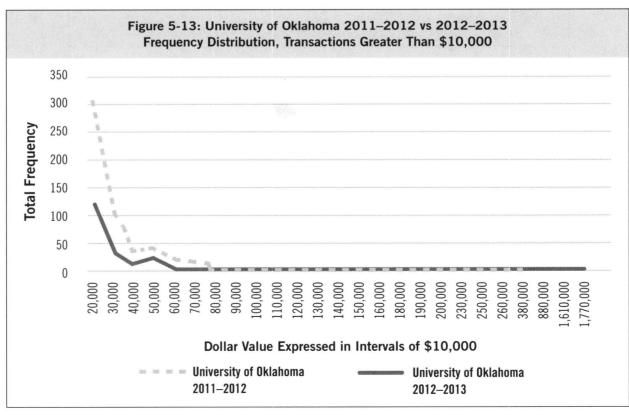

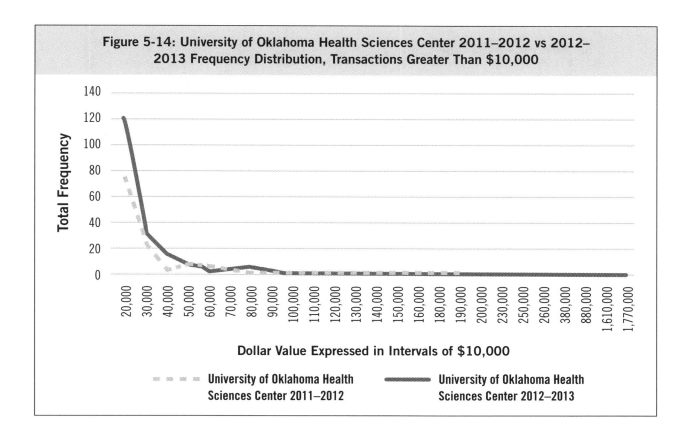

Figure 5-14: University of Oklahoma Health Sciences Center 2011–2012 vs 2012–2013 Frequency Distribution, Transactions Greater Than $10,000

The same pattern is apparent to varying degrees in all three institutions. There were more transactions in 2011–2012 with values between $10,000 and $60,000. For the University of Oklahoma institutions, the tails were longer in 2012–2013.

What is known thus far. The inversion of the frequencies in the tails is unexpected. Even though it did occur in the prior year, it was not as clearly defined as it was in 2012–2013. The large value expenditures are unusual, particularly when compared to 2011–2012. This would mean that four potential high-risk cells may have been found in the 2012–2013 data, those being the transactions greater than $10,000 and less than $60,000 and those greater than $60,000 for the University of Oklahoma and the same range for the University of Oklahoma Health Sciences Center. Splitting the tail at $60,000 is in part due to the length of the tail and the frequencies that now reside in each cell.

The major constraint of frequency analysis is its inability to adequately deal with the hump in the frequency distribution. If the subset is small enough, scanning all of the transactions is a possibility. However, in today's environment of large data sets, even small subsets have a relatively large number of transactions, with the majority of those transactions being located in the hump of the frequency distribution. Time series analysis provides a method to de-aggregate the hump into smaller components by spreading the transactions over equal time intervals. The success of this method of analysis depends on the presence of seasonality or the fluctuation of the frequency of transactions over time as the market in which the business entity competes—moves from highly competitive seasons to the off seasons where business activity such as sales is reduced.

Summary – What's Important

Case Study

- Use the graphical method, measures of central tendency, and tabular format to assess the data.

- Look for where the data diverges from what is expected.

- Areas of interest occur when the lines on the graph representing the benchmark data and the data of concern:

  - ☐ Diverge (separate) from each other,
  - ☐ Cross over (or intersect) each other,
  - ☐ Create different-sized humps, or
  - ☐ Create different lengths in the tails.

Chapter 6

TIME SERIES ANALYSIS

Time series analysis is an analytical procedure that displays transactions over time (often called a trend line). The peaks and valleys in the trend line indicate seasonality in the data—periods of high sales or activity and periods of fewer sales or less activity.

What Is a Time Series Distribution?

A time series distribution is displayed on a two-axis graph in which the vertical axis represents total frequency or total dollar amount and the horizontal axis represents a time period (weekly, biweekly, monthly). Though a computer will perform calculations and graph data, it typically does it by using all of the individual data points as opposed to using time intervals. Similar to a frequency distribution, this results in a great deal of noise or jaggedness in the curve.

Grouping the data into equal time intervals alleviates the problem somewhat so that the curve becomes smoother and the shape of the curve can be determined. However, if the number of time intervals is too small, the shape of the distribution is lost. With practice, the auditor will gain a feeling for the data and choose an appropriate interval width that does not result in too few or too many intervals. The time interval that seems to give the best balance of enough data points without having too much jaggedness in the curve is either biweekly or monthly. There is no restriction on the number of time intervals. The auditor can chose a six-month, 12-month, or 24-month period. The only constraint is that the curve must display seasonality. **Figure 6-1**, **figure 6-2**, and **figure 6-3** depict a common seasonality pattern.

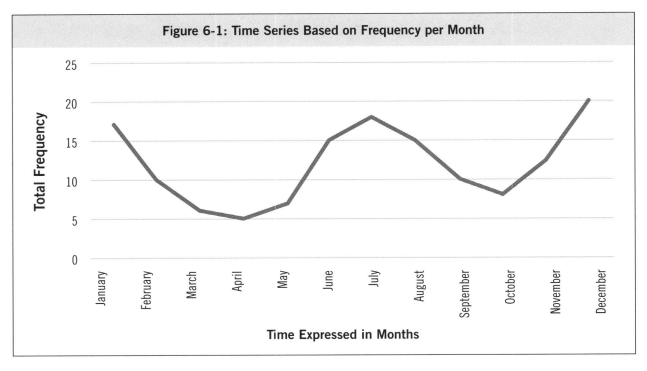

Figure 6-1: Time Series Based on Frequency per Month

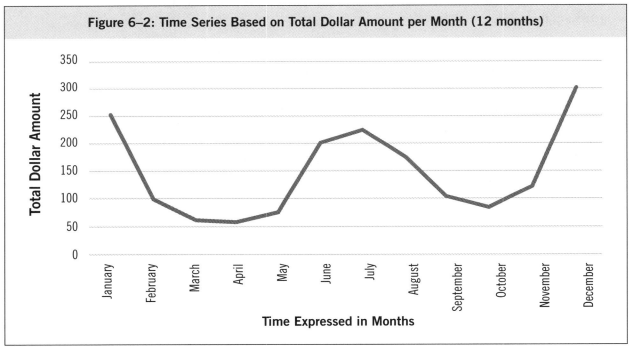

Figure 6–2: Time Series Based on Total Dollar Amount per Month (12 months)

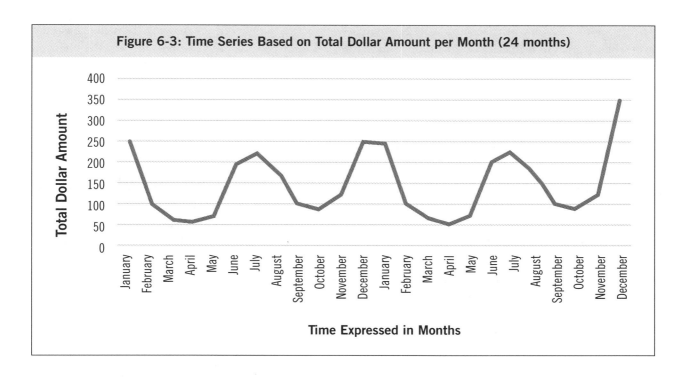

Figure 6-3: Time Series Based on Total Dollar Amount per Month (24 months)

Note that the curves follow roughly the same shape. Time series based on dollar amount may have more sharply defined peaks and valleys because there is not a one-to-one correspondence between frequency and dollar amount, hence the variations in dollar amounts sometimes accentuates the seasonality.

The peaks represent periods of high business activity such as increased sales, expenditures, or revenue growth. The valleys indicate periods when the market is depressed or when sales and business activity are reduced. Note that this is a natural pattern for most businesses. There are periods in any market segment when activity is at a high level and other periods when the activity is naturally reduced. The shape of the seasonality curve is unique to the nature of the business entity. There is not a single seasonality curve for all businesses, rather business entities that compete in the same market segment will have similar seasonality curves. Business entities that compete in different industries or different market segments will have different seasonality curves.

Time series does not have the variety of curves that is seen in frequency analysis (such as uniform, skewed, or bimodal) and it does not use the measures of central tendency to distinguish between various curve shapes. Instead, time series has only a single curve, commonly called a seasonality or trend curve. Both labels intentionally refer to changes in the curve over time. The statistical metric employed in time series analysis is the correlation.

Why Is Seasonality Important?

In frequency analysis, the expectation of the auditor is to see a skewed distribution for financial data. The shape of the curve is part of the auditor's expectation. When that shape is not apparent, or if it is there but does not match the expected shape seen in the benchmark, then the auditor should question why that is the case. Similarly in time series, the auditor should expect to see seasonality. If seasonality is not present, or the seasonality does not match the seasonality in the benchmark, the auditor should question why that is the case.

There is another reason why time series analysis is used in conjunction with frequency analysis. The major constraint in frequency analysis is the size of the hump. Subdivision will only go so far and consequently the frequency in the hump may still be fairly large. Time series plots the transactions based on date of occurrence. Shifting to a time perspective allows the auditor to de-aggregate the hump to some extent by spreading the transactions out over the time periods involved rather than lumping them together based on dollar value.

Correlation

The correlation is an index of a relationship between two variables or columns of data. In order to consider the measurement of a relationship between two variables, or in this instance, the relationship between a benchmark data set and a data set of concern, there must first be a defined, logical, and easily defensible relationship between the data in the two different data sets. In this instance, the relationship is based on time, or to be more specific, the time interval used in the time series analysis. The frequency or dollar information is totaled over the selected time interval. Frequency totals or total dollar amounts are paired up with their respective values in the other data set based on using exactly the same time interval. For example, if month was used as the time interval, the total frequency of transactions for January in the benchmark data would be paired with the total frequency of transactions for January in the data set of concern. This pairwise relationship *must* be established if the calculated correlation is to have any meaning.

The Pearson product moment coefficient of correlation (r) is one of the most frequently used correlations. The calculated values of the correlation range from minus 1 to positive 1. The sign (negative or positive) and the size of the value are both important to interpret the correlation. The sign is indicative of the direction of the relationship between the two variables. A negative value means that as one variable increases, the other decreases. A positive value means that as one variable increases, the other also increases. With respect to size, the closer to zero, the relationship between the two variables is considered to be weaker. When close to 1 (or -1), the relationship between the two variables is considered to be strong. **Table 6-1** provides more explicit values for determining the strength of the relationship. Note that if the benchmark trend line matched the trend line from the data set of concern, a strong positive correlation would result.

Table 6-1: Strength of Relationship Between Two Variables (Pearson r Correlation)	
0 to .2	No relationship
.2 to .4	Weak relationship
.5 to .7	Moderate relationship
.8 to 1	Strong relationship

Note the values are expressed as absolute values (a similar relationship would appear with negative values).

Variance in Common (r²)

Even with the considerations of direction of the relationship (negative or positive) and size of the correlation (nonexistent to strong), the correlation (r) is still difficult to interpret from the perspective of pinpointing the exact relationship between the two sets of data. However, the r^2 value has a different quality. It refers to the proportion of variance in one variable that is explained by the variance in the other variable. Another way of looking at r^2 is the proportion of variance that is in common between the two variables. Having a large portion of variance in common would indicate that the two columns of data are very similar. For low values of r, r^2 is also very low. As r increases in size, r^2 also increases in size but at a greater rate than r (Keith, 1972). A high value of r^2 would be expected if the benchmark data trend line matched the trend line from the data set of concern.

Scatter Plots

Unlike line graphs that have been illustrated thus far, in scatter plots, the axis represents the variable or data set. For the purposes of analytical procedures, one axis will represent the benchmark data and the other the data set of concern.

Scatter plots are useful because the shape of data points around the line of best fit to the data will indicate the direction of the relationship (positive or negative) and the strength of the relationship (none, weak, moderate, or strong). The *line of best fit* is a line that could be statistically calculated using the least squares method of estimation (linear regression). It is a line that is situated in such a way that the distance from the data points to the line is kept to a minimum. This line, particularly in time series analysis, is eyeballed as opposed to calculated. The line is deliberately positioned to align with the majority of the data points so that the position of the outliers is emphasized. The major advantage of scatter plots is the ability to identify outliers in the time series data (i.e., those data points farthest from the line of best fit).

The first figure illustrates a scatter plot in which the pattern of the data points does not fall close to a line of best fit. In fact, almost any line would be considered an equally good candidate as a line of best fit. This is an example of little to no relationship between the benchmark data set and the data set of concern. In **figure 6-4** there are two potential lines that could be best fit. If the relationship is not obvious, then it is likely not very strong.

In the next graph, the line of best fit originates in the lower left and extends to the upper right. A positive relationship (as values in the benchmark data increase, so do the values in the data set of concern) exists when the line of best fit is oriented from the lower left to the upper right, as seen in **figure 6-5**.

A negative relationship occurs when the line of best of best fit is oriented from the upper left to the lower right (see **figure 6-6**). In this instance, as values in the benchmark data set increase, values in the data set of concern would decrease.

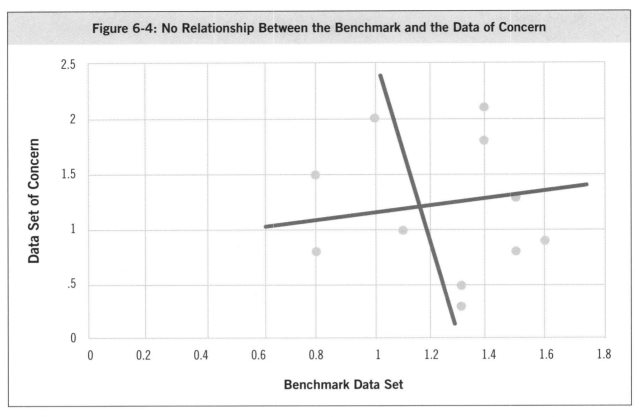

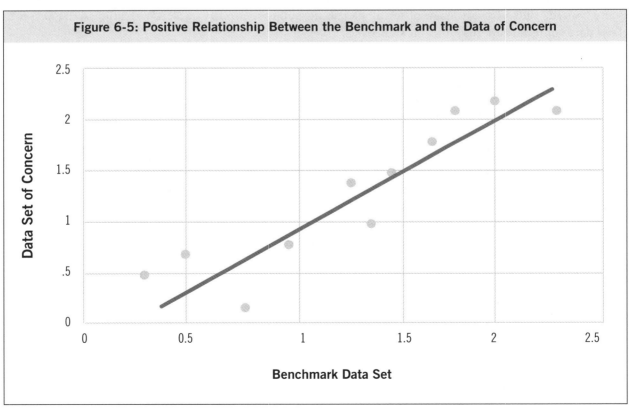

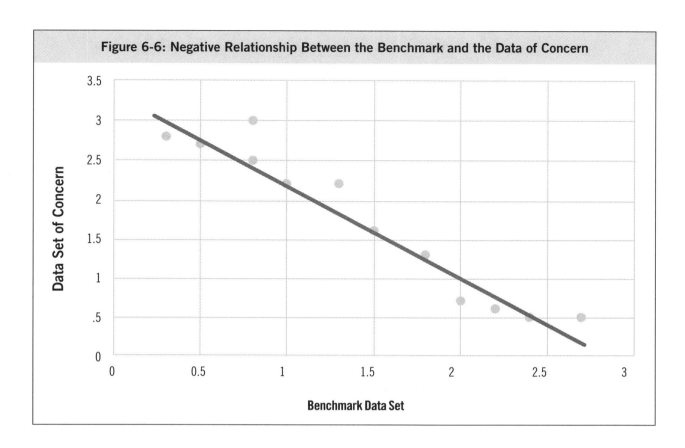

The size or value of the correlation can also be estimated from the scatter plot. To perform this estimation, lines must be drawn from the data points to the line of best fit in such a way that the drawn line is perpendicular to the line of best fit (see **figure 6-7**).

The dropped perpendiculars are representative of variance. When the lengths of the dropped perpendiculars are large, the variance is also large, thus resulting in a weaker correlation with a lower numerical value (for example, .2 to .4). When the lengths of the dropped perpendiculars are small, the variance is also small, resulting in a stronger correlation with a higher calculated value (for example, .8 or .9).

For the purposes of the analytical procedures, just as in frequency analysis, the expectation is that the time series graphs for the benchmark data will track very closely to the data of concern. If this is the case, then strong positive correlations are expected. In a scatter plot, this would be portrayed by a line of best fit going from the lower left to the upper right, with dropped perpendiculars that are relatively short in length.

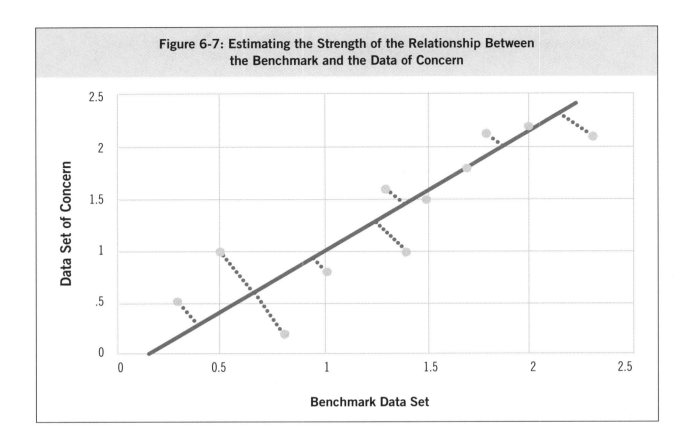

Figure 6-7: Estimating the Strength of the Relationship Between the Benchmark and the Data of Concern

Differentiating Between the Benchmark Data Set and the Data Set of Concern

Remember that the benchmark data set was selected as a suitable comparison because it was deemed to be low risk. If the data set of concern is also low risk, then when the two sets of data are graphed, the curves should be very similar. For the statistical metric, the correlation would exhibit a strong positive value. When the lines diverge, the correlation is weakened and the difference is assumed to be driven by risk because the subdivision of the data set was based on risk.

Figure 6-8 demonstrates what is meant by little difference between the two distributions. Note the high positive correlation (very close to 1) and the high variance in common (r^2 = .976).

The strong positive correlation is reflected in the scatter plot, which originates in the lower left and moves to the upper right (see **figure 6-9**). Note how close the data points are to the line of best fit. This would indicate that the variance is very low and there is a strong relationship between the benchmark data and the data of concern.

Figure 6-10 and **figure 6-11** illustrate two examples in which the benchmark data does not match the data set of concern. The first curve has an increase of frequency of transactions in a valley and a peak during the time frame from March to July. The divergence from the benchmark data results in a lower correlation (r = .792), which is now out of the strong positive range (above .8). The variance in common is 62.7%, which is not overly high, particularly compared to the previous example of 97.6%.

The scatter plot also demonstrates divergence for the data points that are farthest from the line of best fit.

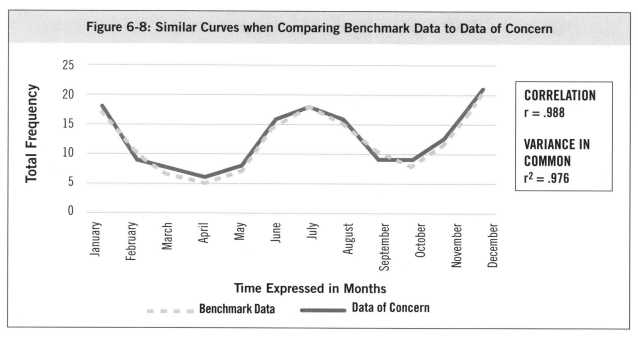

Figure 6-8: Similar Curves when Comparing Benchmark Data to Data of Concern

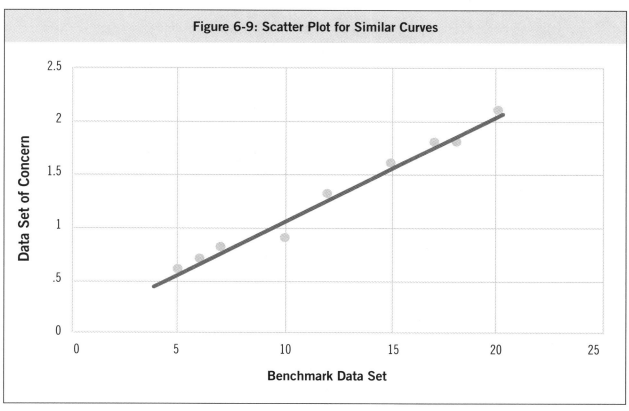

Figure 6-9: Scatter Plot for Similar Curves

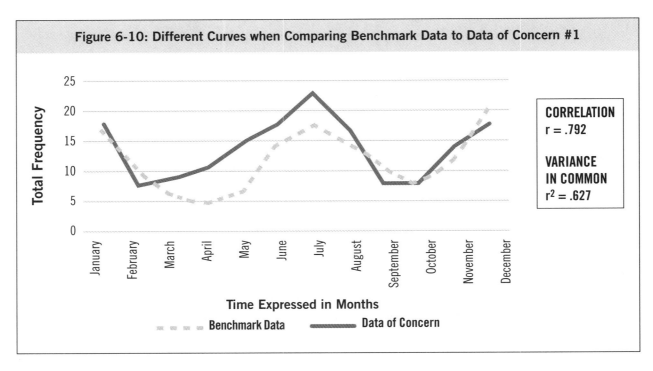

Figure 6-10: Different Curves when Comparing Benchmark Data to Data of Concern #1

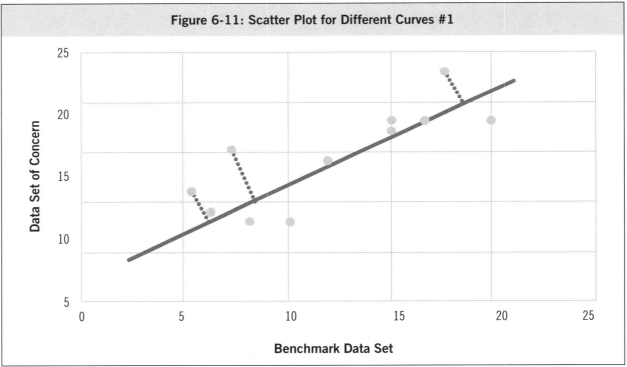

Figure 6-11: Scatter Plot for Different Curves #1

There are three data points that are the farthest from the line of best fit. Remember that the relationship between the benchmark data set and the data set of concern is based on the time intervals. Each of the points in the scatter plot in **figure 6-11** represents a specific month. The ones with the largest distance from the line of best fit have dropped perpendiculars. In order from left to right, the three months corresponding to the above data points are April, May, and July. These three months have the largest deviation from the benchmark data. Is this a hard and fast method to determine a problem area? Likely not, but the intent is that it is a good place to start looking.

In **figure 6-12**, the curves diverge in May and the benchmark data appears to lag behind the data of concern. If there had been a true lag variable affecting the difference between the benchmark data and the data of concern, the lag effect would be apparent throughout the 12 months, not just in the latter six months. There is a moderate correlation when a much stronger correlation would be expected and the variance in common is also moderate at 50.3%.

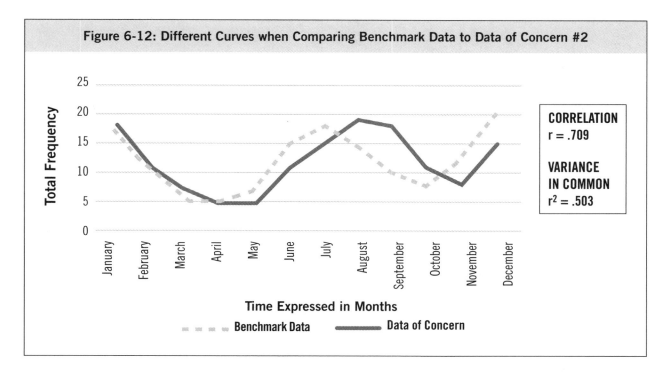

The scatter plot for the second example of different curves is illustrated in **figure 6-13**. The dropped perpendiculars moving left to right represent September and August, the months with the largest deviation from the benchmark data set.

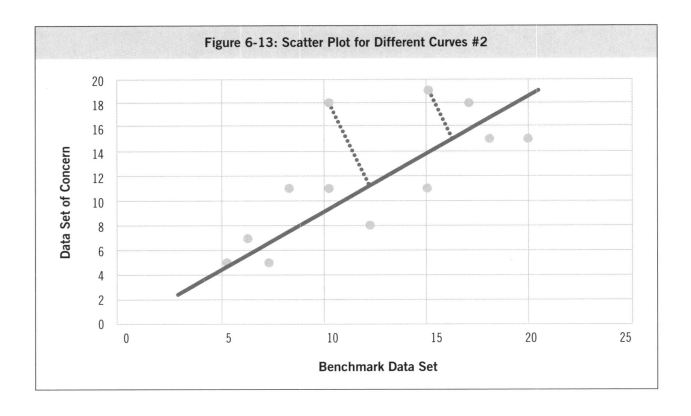

Figure 6-13: Scatter Plot for Different Curves #2

Summary – What's Important

- Time series analysis depends on a trend graph to depict seasonality in the data. The peaks and valleys that define seasonality are used to help de-aggregate the hump in the frequency analysis.

- When the benchmark trend curve tracks very closely to the data of concern trend curve, a strong positive correlation will be evident with high proportion of the variance in common.

- When the two curves deviate from each other or cross each other, the correlation is lower, as is the proportion of variance in common.

- The scatter plots demonstrate how close the data points lie to the line of best fit. Scatter plots are useful in identifying outliers that correspond to the points with the widest divergence in the trend graphs.

- Trend graphs can be calculated based on total frequency of transactions or items in a given time period, or total dollar amount in a given time period.

- Using total dollar amount typically increases the amount of variance, thus reducing the strength of the relationship. However, this should not stop auditors from looking at the total dollar amount because patterns in expenditures may still be evident.

Chapter 7

TIME SERIES CASE STUDY

The data set has already been prepared and the auditor has had some experience with pivot tables to create frequency distributions. Note that there is no need to change the benchmark for the time series analysis. Below are the instructions to create a 15-day time interval (two weeks). Also included are instructions for a 7-day interval, a 5-day interval, and a 3-day interval.

Activity or Metric	Excel Function	Instructions
Creating intervals for time series analysis - month year interval	Re-format a date column into month/year	Copy the date data into a separate column.
		Place your cursor on the first cell in the column, right click and select format cells.
		Select "Custom." Scroll down and select "mmm-yy."
		Copy and paste onto the complete column.
Creating intervals for time series analysis - 15-day interval	"=IF(DAY(C2)<=15,DATE(YEAR(C2),MONTH(C2),15),EOMONTH(C2,0))"	Sort the date data in chronological sequence.
		Choose a time interval that is small enough to allow you to see seasonality. In this instance, a two-week interval is used.
		Select the column in which you will be creating the interval labels. Go to format, select date, and chose the date format you wish to use.
		In the first cell of the column adjacent to the column containing the date data, type the following: "=IF(DAY(C2)<=15,DATE(YEAR(C2),MONTH(C2),15),EOMONTH(C2,0))." C2 refers to the cell in which the first date data is located. Copy the formula and then paste it into all of the cells in the column adjacent to the column containing the date data so that every cell in the dollar data column has the formula pasted beside it.

Activity or Metric	Excel Function	Instructions
Creating intervals for time series analysis – 7-day interval	"=IF(DAY(B2)<=7,DATE(YEAR(B2),MONTH(B2),7),IF(AND(DAY(B2)>7,DAY(B2)<=14),DATE(YEAR(B2),MONTH(B2),14),IF(AND(DAY(B2)>14,DAY(B2)<=21),DATE(YEAR(B2),MONTH(B2),21),IF(AND(DAY(B2)>21,DAY(B2)<=31),EOMONTH(B2,0)))))"	Follow the same instructions as the 15-day interval, except use the 7-day interval formula. B2 refers to the cell in which the first date data is located.
Creating intervals for time series analysis – 5-day interval	"=IF(DAY(M2)<=5,DATE(YEAR(M2),MONTH(M2),5),IF(AND(DAY(M2)>5,DAY(M2)<=10),DATE(YEAR(M2),MONTH(M2),10),IF(AND(DAY(M2)>10,DAY(M2)<=15),DATE(YEAR(M2),MONTH(M2),15),IF(AND(DAY(M2)>15,DAY(M2)<=20),DATE(YEAR(M2),MONTH(M2),20),IF(AND(DAY(M2)>20,DAY(M2)<=25),DATE(YEAR(M2),MONTH(M2),25),EOMONTH(M2,0))))))"	Follow the same instructions as the 15-day interval, except use the 5-day interval formula. M2 refers to the cell in which the first date data is located.
Creating intervals for time series analysis – 3-day interval	"=IF(DAY(F2)<=3,DATE(YEAR(F2),MONTH(F2),3),IF(AND(DAY(F2)>3,DAY(F2)<=6),DATE(YEAR(F2),MONTH(F2),6),IF(AND(DAY(F2)>6,DAY(F2)<=9),DATE(YEAR(F2),MONTH(F2),9),IF(AND(DAY(F2)>9,DAY(F2)<=12),DATE(YEAR(F2),MONTH(F2),12),IF(AND(DAY(F2)>12,DAY(F2)<=15),DATE(YEAR(F2),MONTH(F2),15),IF(AND(DAY(F2)>15,DAY(F2)<=18),DATE(YEAR(F2),MONTH(F2),18),IF(AND(DAY(F2)>18,DAY(F2)<=21),DATE(YEAR(F2),MONTH(F2),21),IF(AND(DAY(F2)>21,DAY(F2)<=24),DATE(YEAR(F2),MONTH(F2),24),IF(AND(DAY(F2)>24,DAY(F2)<=27),DATE(YEAR(F2),MONTH(F2),27),EOMONTH(F2,0)))))))))))"	Follow the same instructions as the 15-day interval, except use the 3-day interval formula. F2 refers to the cell in which the first date data is located.

The following instructions demonstrate the use of the time intervals in a pivot table to complete a time series analysis. It is done in exactly the same manner as the frequency analysis.

Activity or Metric	Excel Function	Instructions
Calculating the total dollar value and total frequency within each of the specified time intervals	Pivot Tables	Highlight/select all cells you wish to examine in the subset, including column headings. To do this, click on a single cell in the data set, then press Ctrl A. Note that if you are doing several pivot tables in the same spreadsheet, separate the rows and cut and paste the column headings for each subdivision. This makes it easier to identify which columns and rows you wish to select.
		Click on the Insert tab in the toolbar at the top of the spreadsheet. Select Pivot Table (upper left corner). A dialog box will appear. The selected cells (using the column labels) are pre-populated in the upper portion of the box.
		In the lower portion, select Existing Worksheet and input a cell (e.g., i25 – with column and row identifier) that is to the right of the columns you are examining where you would like the pivot table to appear on your worksheet. Click on Okay.
		(continued)

Activity or Metric	Excel Function	Instructions
		A dialog box will appear to the far right of your screen. If you scroll over to the right, you will see a space marked for the location of the pivot table.

In the upper portion of the dialog box (Pivot Table Field List) will be a list of the column headings. Select the dollar value column, the name column, and the interval name column.

In the lower portion of the dialog box, the interval name column will appear as a row label. The dollar value appears to the right in the sum box. This will provide a sum for the dollar values within each of the interval names. Drag the Name Column from the upper portion of the dialog box to the sum box. This will provide a frequency count of the number of times the name appears in each interval. If there is more than one name, the pivot table will subdivide to show separate frequency counts.

The pivot table will appear on your spreadsheet as the above actions are performed. |

The Pearson r correlation is found in the same location as the mean, median, and mode. The manner in which the data is identified is the same, except that the correlation requires two sets of data as opposed to one.

Activity or Metric	Excel Function	Instructions
Pearson r Correlation	CORREL	Go to the Formulas tab and select More Functions - Statistical. Scroll down and select CORREL.

The dialog box will prompt you to type in the two arrays of the data you wish to correlate. In the Array 1 section, type in the first cell of your data and the last cell of your data, separated by a colon (a2:a407). In the Array 2, type in the first cell and last cell of the second set of data using the same format as the Data Array (b2:b22). Press Okay. |

The scatter plot is graphed in the same manner as the line graphs for frequency analysis and time series analysis. The scatter plot icon is located slightly to the right of the line graph icon. Pay attention to the axis labels. When you enter the data for the scatter plot, the column on the left is associated with the horizontal axis. The column to the right is associated with the vertical axis.

Activity or Metric	Excel Function	Instructions
Graphing a Scatter Plot	Insert/Graph Type	Because the data from the benchmark data set and the data set of concern is typically in different spreadsheets, the auditor must first create the appropriate columns of data and then cut and paste them so that they are side by side and matched up based on their time intervals.

Highlight the two columns of data, click Insert, select the appropriate graph, and click on its icon. |

Become Familiar with the Market Conditions: State of Oklahoma

Fortunately, the State of Oklahoma data has a column labeled Year Month, which means there is a time interval that has already been created. **Figure 7-1** depicts the overall trend in frequency of P-Card expenditures by month over the fiscal year 2012–2013.

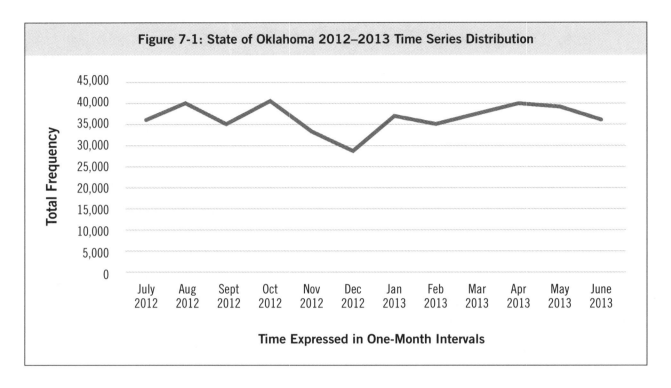

Note the dip in June/July, September, and December, which may be indicative of the changing of semesters. It is these valleys that accentuate the peaks. The trend graph is relatively smooth. To create a trend graph using two-week intervals, the Transaction Date was used to group the transactions into two-week intervals. *It was at this point that it was discovered some of the transaction dates were in different formats and could not be read. A fix was put in place to change the format and a valuable lesson was learned. Live data always presents a challenge to auditors, whether it is dates in different formats or agency names spelled two different ways. Going in prepared for something to go wrong alleviates much of the shock when it happens.*

When the time interval is changed to a two-week period, a slightly different pattern emerges compared to the one-month intervals.

First, note that there are transactions prior to June. In the previous graph, the data was based on the Year Month column. In **figure 7-2**, the data is based on the fixed transaction date. The data indicates that there were prior year P-Card expenditures included in the 2012–2013 fiscal year data.

Second, note that the graph has a more jagged appearance. The downside of reducing the time interval is a loss in smoothness in the curve. On the positive side, the drops in frequency, though slightly less because the same monthly frequency is now spread over two data points, are more specific. The June, end of August, and December drops become more apparent. Note that the drop in February becomes more pronounced.

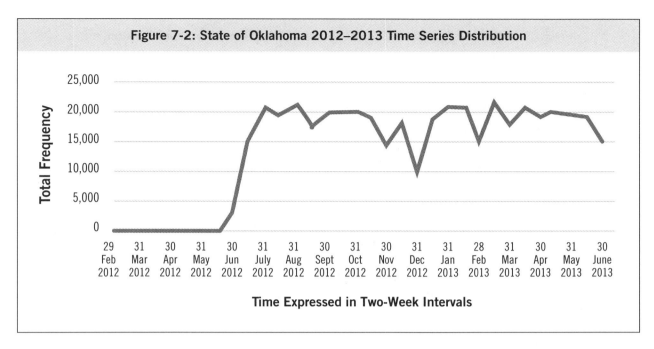

Figure 7-2: State of Oklahoma 2012–2013 Time Series Distribution

Total Frequency (y-axis): 0, 5,000, 10,000, 15,000, 20,000, 25,000

Time Expressed in Two-Week Intervals (x-axis): 29 Feb 2012, 31 Mar 2012, 30 Apr 2012, 31 May 2012, 30 Jun 2012, 31 July 2012, 31 Aug 2012, 30 Sept 2012, 31 Oct 2012, 30 Nov 2012, 31 Dec 2012, 31 Jan 2013, 28 Feb 2013, 31 Mar 2013, 30 Apr 2013, 31 May 2013, 30 June 2013

It was at this point that is was decided to not include data prior to the last two weeks of June for the time series analysis. The majority of the data points were mostly single digit numbers versus the last two weeks of June, which had substantially more transactions. Including this data would detract from the shape of the curve and increase variance, thus reducing the strength of the correlations. The frequencies for the last two weeks of June were large enough not to severely increase variance, yet small enough to increase the range of data for the calculation of the correlation. The relative frequencies and dollar amounts followed a consistent pattern in the data set as a whole and in the relevant subdivisions.

Validate the Internal Benchmark, Prior Year (2011–2012): State of Oklahoma

Comparison with the 2011–2012 benchmark data (using the monthly interval) demonstrates a fairly good match. There is slightly more jaggedness in the 2012–2013 data, yet it still follows the benchmark curve relatively closely. The finding is supported by a moderate correlation of .781 and 61% of the variance in common (see **figure 7-3**).

The scatter plot in **figure 7-4** is grouped together and resides relatively close to the line of best fit. This is again consistent with the above findings. Note that though the data points in the scatter plot are fairly close to the line of best fit, the correlation is still only moderate (.781). The lack of strength in the correlation is due to the fact that the data points do not cover a large range and are therefore grouped more closely together.

In the following analysis (see **figure 7-5**), the transactions with dates prior to June 1st (146 in 2011–2012 and 18 in 2012–2013) were removed so that the graphs illustrated a cleaner relationship. Given that the other time intervals had tens of thousands of transactions, it is highly unlikely that this data influenced the outcome.

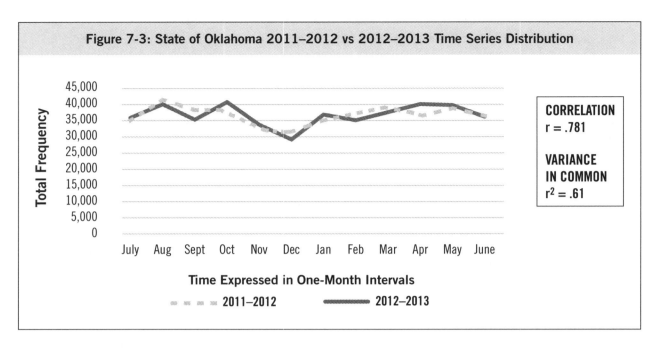

Figure 7-3: State of Oklahoma 2011–2012 vs 2012–2013 Time Series Distribution

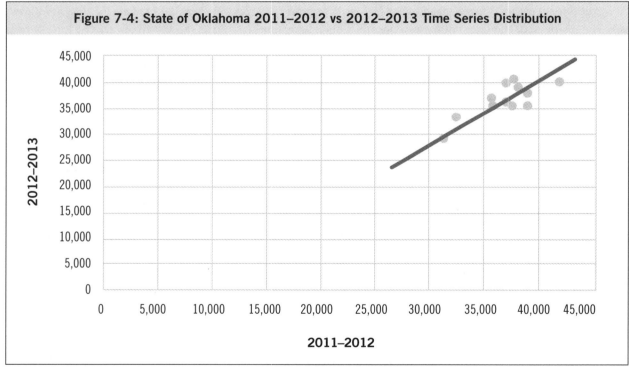

Figure 7-4: State of Oklahoma 2011–2012 vs 2012–2013 Time Series Distribution

The comparison with the benchmark using a smaller time interval (two weeks) illustrates the advantage of smaller intervals (without going too small, which would have too much jaggedness). The curve has stretched out and the original jaggedness is apparent, but the jaggedness is matched by the benchmark. The major dips and peaks line up between the two curves. The correlation has moved up to a .95 with 90.2% of the variance in common between the benchmark and the data of concern.

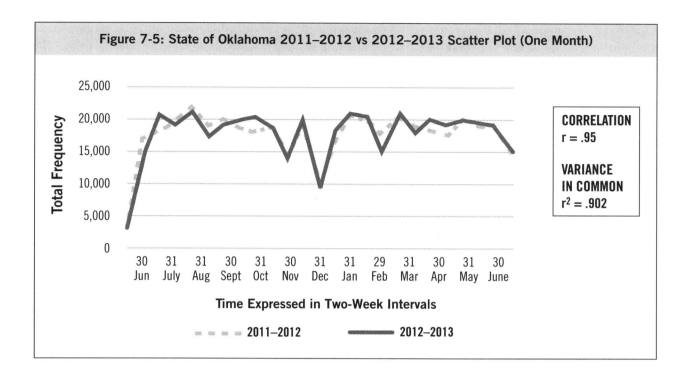

Figure 7-5: State of Oklahoma 2011–2012 vs 2012–2013 Scatter Plot (One Month)

One of the reasons that the correlation is stronger is that there is a larger range in the data points. This can be seen in the scatter plot in **figure 7-6**. The stretching out of the data points (a larger range in values) allows for a much better fit to the line of best fit.

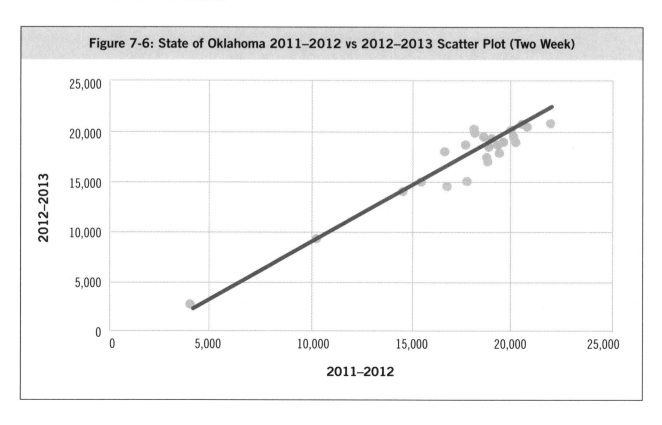

Figure 7-6: State of Oklahoma 2011–2012 vs 2012–2013 Scatter Plot (Two Week)

One of the advantages of time series analysis is that it can be done on total dollar amount per time interval in addition to total frequency (see **figure 7-7**). The comparison is done in exactly the same manner as above. The separation in the lines representing the benchmark and data of concern can be seen in July, August, September, and December. It is this type of divergence that brings the correlation down and subsequently lessens the variance in common. Remember that there is not a one-to-one correspondence between dollar amounts and frequency. As a result, there is typically more divergence between the lines.

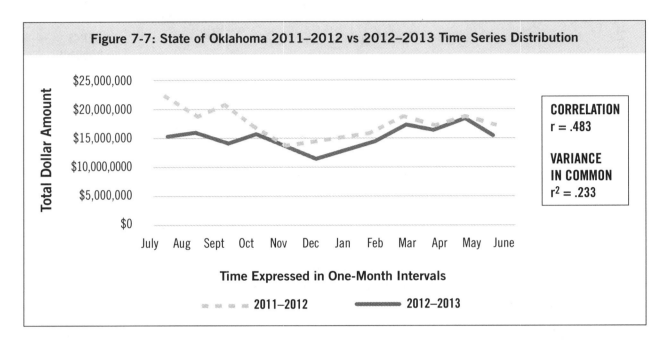

In the scatter plot in **figure 7-8**, the data points are clustered together with the lack of range counterbalancing the closeness to the line of best fit. The data point with the dropped perpendicular closest to the left is from September and the other is from July, which coincides with the data points with the largest divergence in the time series distribution above.

Similar to the time series analysis using total frequency of transactions, those transactions prior to June 15 were removed to help clarify the pattern in the graph and scatter plot. Combining both debits and credits in 2012–2013 amounted to a credit of $822.88.

In the previous analysis (**figure 7-7**), a one-month period was used in the time series analysis. In this analysis, the time period has been reduced to two-week intervals. As can be seen in **figure 7-9**, there is a more-jagged curve in the benchmark data. This could have just as easily been in the 2012–2013 data. The increased variation is in part due to the reduction of the time interval. However, there is another factor present. Consider **figure 7-5**, the time series graph for the same data but using total frequency over the two-week period as opposed to total dollar amount. Note that the total frequency line graphs are a very close match producing a correlation of .95 and variance in common of 90.2%. In **figure 7-9**, the match to the benchmark is much less pronounced, resulting in a lower correlation of .589 and only 34.7% of the variance in common.

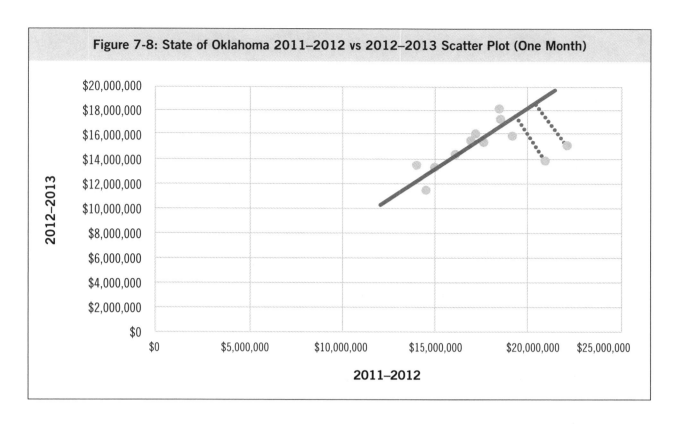

Figure 7-8: State of Oklahoma 2011–2012 vs 2012–2013 Scatter Plot (One Month)

This is due to the fact that there is not a one-to-one match between frequency and dollar value. For example, a difference in frequency of five transactions from one time interval to another would be portrayed identically no matter where in the time distribution it occurred. The same five transactions could have a total dollar value of $50 or $50,000.00. The lack of a one-to-one correspondence between frequency and dollar value increases the variance in the dollar value data.

The increased variation in the time series distribution using total dollar amounts should not deter an auditor from looking at the data in this manner. Large fluctuations in the line graph can also indicate dollar amounts that may be problematic.

The scatter plot in **figure 7-10** has a cluster of data points that are elliptical in shape. The outliers, however, pull the line of best fit from the cluster. Note that the data points with the dropped perpendiculars correspond to the first two weeks of July, the first two weeks of August, and the last two weeks of September.

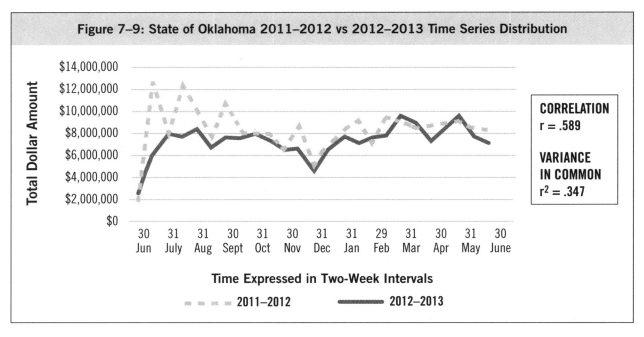

Figure 7–9: State of Oklahoma 2011–2012 vs 2012–2013 Time Series Distribution

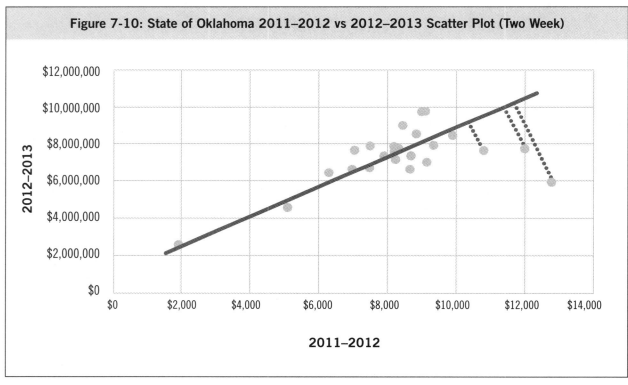

Figure 7-10: State of Oklahoma 2011–2012 vs 2012–2013 Scatter Plot (Two Week)

Validate the External Benchmark: Oklahoma State University (Total Frequency)

The external benchmark—Oklahoma State University—will be subjected to the same analysis, which will ensure that it is also trending as expected. Oklahoma State University is first compared to the prior year using a one-month time interval. The shapes of the two curves match fairly well, with a correlation of .837 and 70.1% of their variance in common (see **figure 7-11**).

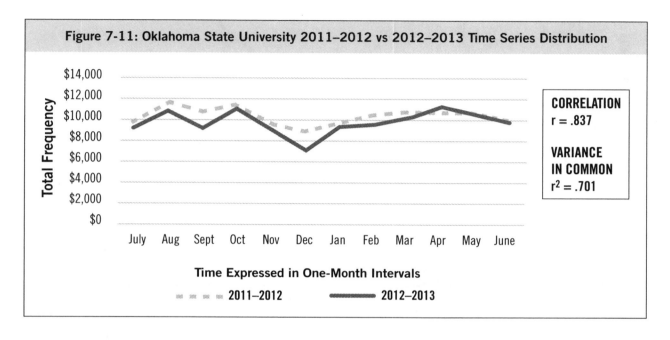

Figure 7-11: Oklahoma State University 2011–2012 vs 2012–2013 Time Series Distribution

As can be seen in the scatter plot in **figure 7-12**, the data points cluster around the line of best fit, also supporting the strong relationship between the 2011–2012 data and the 2012–2013 data.

With the reduction in the time interval to a two-week period, the two curves continue to follow similar patterns (see **figure 7-13**). The correlation has increased to .942 and the variance in common has increased to 88.7%.

The scatter plot in **figure 7-14** demonstrates a very good fit to the estimated regression line, with no data points standing too far off the line.

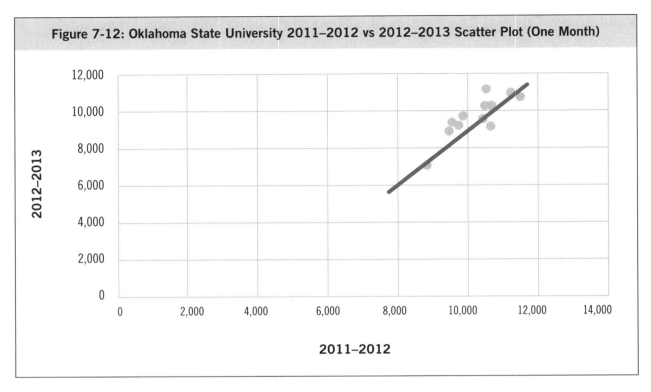

Figure 7-12: Oklahoma State University 2011–2012 vs 2012–2013 Scatter Plot (One Month)

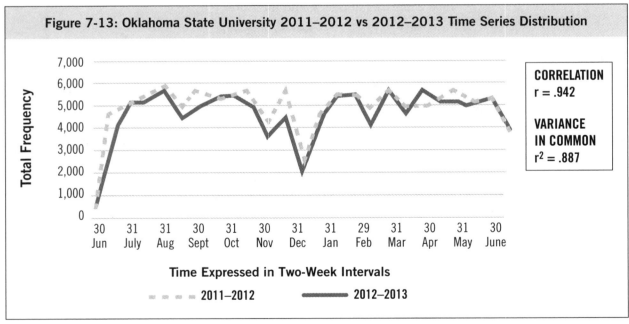

Figure 7-13: Oklahoma State University 2011–2012 vs 2012–2013 Time Series Distribution

CORRELATION
r = .942

VARIANCE
IN COMMON
r^2 = .887

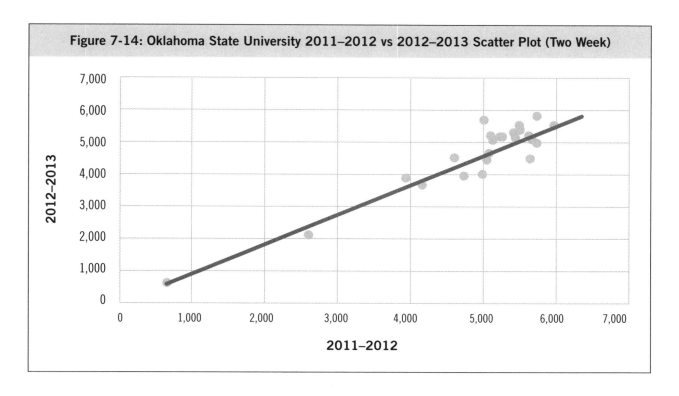

Figure 7-14: Oklahoma State University 2011–2012 vs 2012–2013 Scatter Plot (Two Week)

What is known thus far. With respect to frequency of P-Card transactions, Oklahoma State University has a strong relationship to the prior year benchmark both at the one-month and two-week intervals. This would support the selection of Oklahoma State University as an external benchmark.

Comparison to the Internal Benchmark, Prior Year (2011–2012): University of Oklahoma and University of Oklahoma Health Sciences Center (Total Frequency)

The University of Oklahoma and the University of Oklahoma Health Sciences Center were subjected to the same analysis as Oklahoma State University. At the one-month time interval, the University of Oklahoma had a moderate correlation of .74 with prior year and variance in common of 54.8%. The divergence between the two curves can be seen in August, September, and then December onward (see **figure 7-15**).

The scatter plot in **figure 7-16** shows the data points clustered around the line of best fit, yet the small range of the values in the two variables (2011–2012 and 2012–2013) likely served to bring the correlation down. There are not many points that are very close to the line. About half are some distance from the line, but none are extremely far from the line. The correlation is in the moderate range.

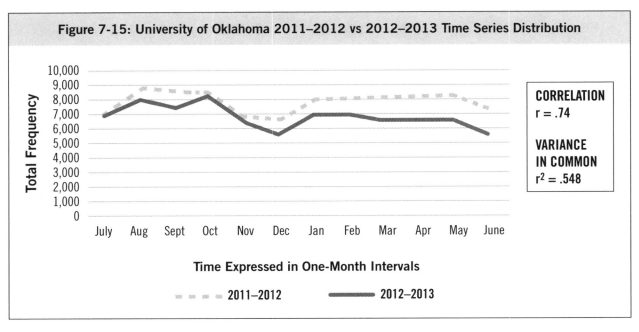

Figure 7-15: University of Oklahoma 2011–2012 vs 2012–2013 Time Series Distribution

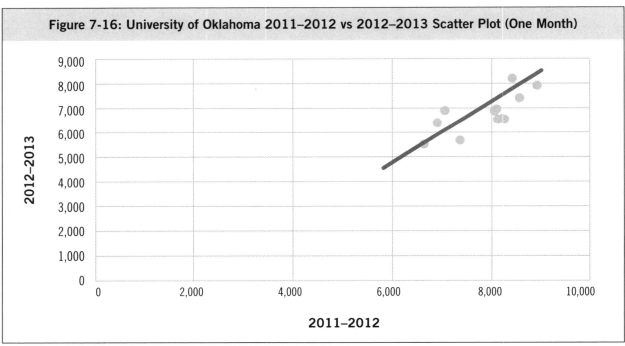

Figure 7-16: University of Oklahoma 2011–2012 vs 2012–2013 Scatter Plot (One Month)

Reducing the time interval to a two-week period increased the correlation to almost the same level as Oklahoma State University (.942 vs .914), with a variance in common of 83.5%. The reduction in the time interval increases the number of data points that are moving in the same direction as the benchmark, which serves to strengthen the correlation (see **figure 7-17**).

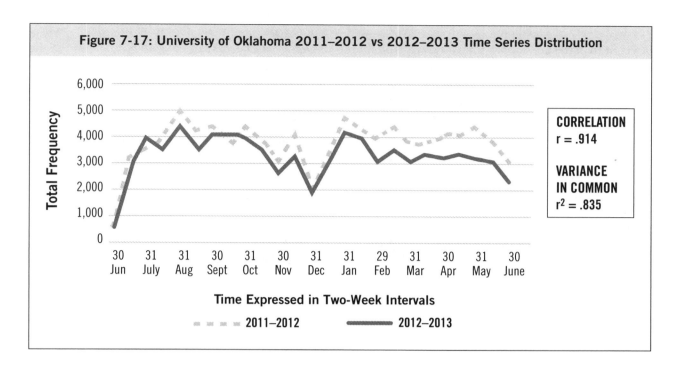

The scatter plot in **figure 7-18** shows data points falling close to the line of best fit, with none standing out as strong outliers.

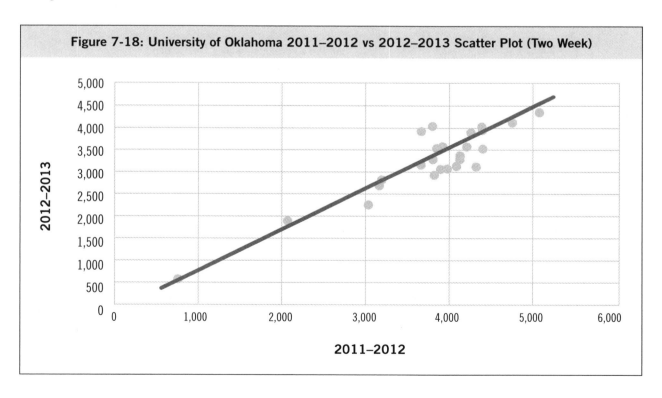

The University of Oklahoma Health Sciences Center has a time series graph that appears at first glance to be a better fit than the one-month time interval graph for the University of Oklahoma (see **figure 7-19**). However, the correlation is markedly lower (.577 versus .74) and a variance in common of 33.3%. Note that though the two curves for the University of Oklahoma in **figure 7-15** are slightly separated, they track each other markedly well. In other words, when the prior year data increases, so does the 2012–2013 data. As can be seen in the University of Oklahoma Health Sciences Center data, though the lines are closer together, they do not track as well, with one curve going up while the other goes down. It is this factor that plays an important role in decreasing the strength of a correlation. Having two curves that are close together is not sufficient to guarantee a strong correlation, which leads to another interesting finding. Particularly when two curves lie very close to each other, the only way to check the strength of the apparent relationship is to calculate the correlation.

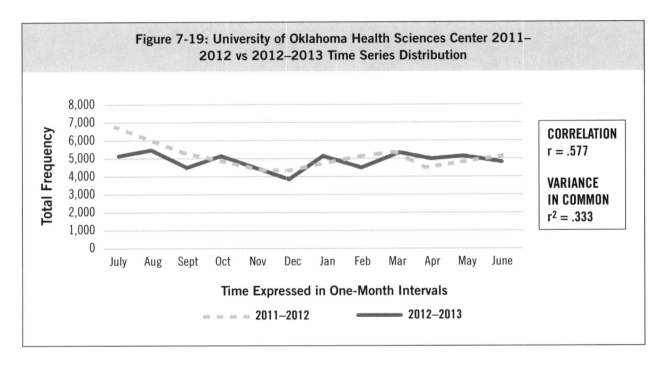

The scatter plot in **figure 7-20** illustrates data points relatively close to the line of best fit. The outlier with the dropped perpendicular is for the month of July.

Decreasing the time interval to two weeks increased the correlation but not to the extent seen in Oklahoma State University or the University of Oklahoma. The correlation remains at moderate with a value of .782 and a variance in common of 61.2% (see **figure 7-21**).

The scatter plot in **figure 7-22** has two outliers, identified with dropped perpendiculars. Those data points correspond to the last two weeks of June (from the prior year) and the first two weeks of July.

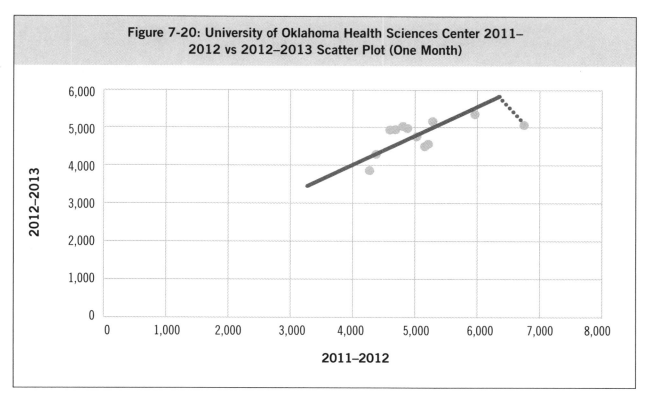

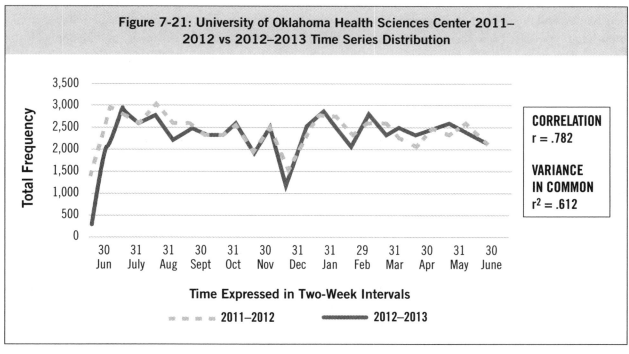

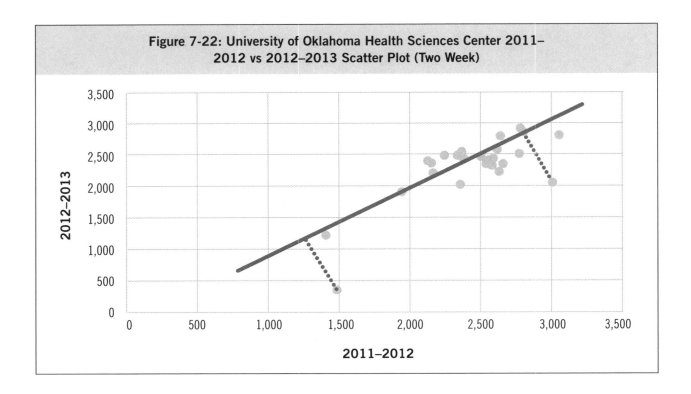

Figure 7-22: University of Oklahoma Health Sciences Center 2011–2012 vs 2012–2013 Scatter Plot (Two Week)

What is known thus far. The University of Oklahoma has a moderately strong relationship with the prior year benchmark, and the strength of that relationship increases to very strong when the time interval is reduced from a month to two weeks. There are no outliers that stand out in the scatter plots. The University of Oklahoma Health Sciences Center has a moderately weak relationship with 2011–2012, and this relationship increases slightly to a moderate relationship when the time interval is decreased from one month to two weeks. The last two weeks of June (prior year) and the first two weeks of July had fewer transactions than in the prior year.

Comparison to the External Benchmark: Oklahoma State University (Total Frequency)

Figure 7-23 illustrates the trend lines for the three educational institutions over one-month time intervals in 2012–2013. At first glance, the curves appear roughly parallel trending in the same direction. Drops in frequency in July, September, and December can be seen. The correlations paint a slightly different picture. The relationship between Oklahoma State University and the University of Oklahoma is only weakly moderate. There is a stronger relationship with the University of Oklahoma Health Sciences Center. The correlation between the University of Oklahoma and the University of Oklahoma Health Sciences Center is listed in part for completeness and in part as an additional piece of information. One would expect that these two institutions would have relatively the same spending patterns given that they belong to the same business entity. The relationship should be at least as strong as that with Oklahoma State University, which is a separate business entity. At the one-month interval, the correlations do not support this assumption (see **table 7-1**).

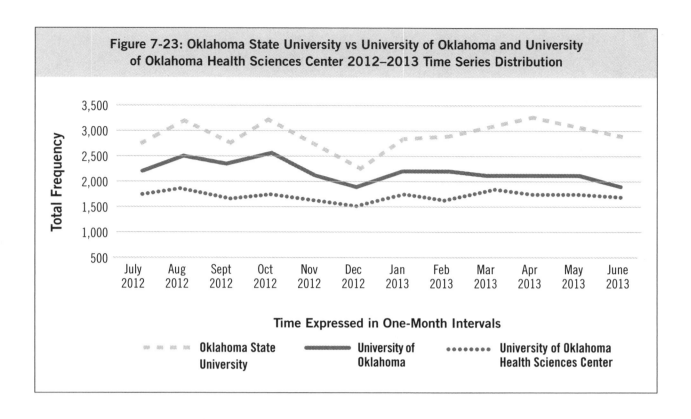

Figure 7-23: Oklahoma State University vs University of Oklahoma and University of Oklahoma Health Sciences Center 2012–2013 Time Series Distribution

Table 7-1: Oklahoma State University vs University of Oklahoma and University of Oklahoma Health Sciences Center 2012–2013 Correlations (Total Frequency over One-Month Time Interval)	Correlation (r)	Variance in Common (r²)
Oklahoma State University vs University of Oklahoma	0.576	0.332
Oklahoma State University vs University of Oklahoma Health Sciences Center	0.821	0.674
University of Oklahoma vs University of Oklahoma Health Sciences Center	0.547	0.299

The scatter plots in **figure 7-24**, **figure 7-25**, and **figure 7-26** were produced for each pair of institutions for which correlations were calculated.

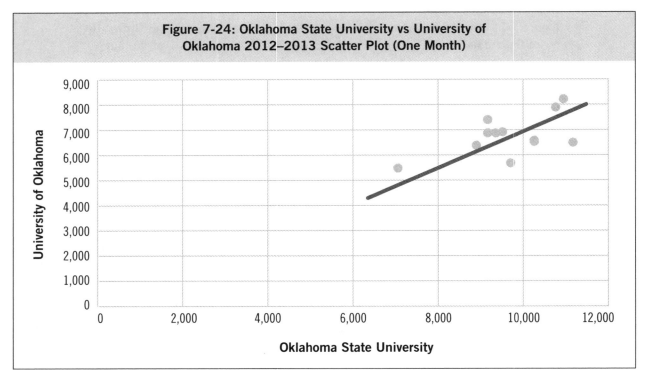

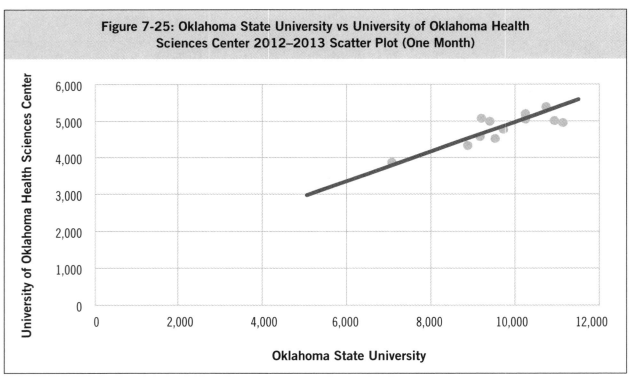

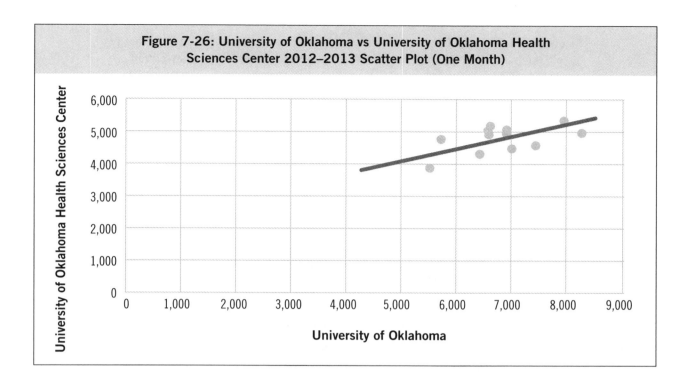

Figure 7-26: University of Oklahoma vs University of Oklahoma Health Sciences Center 2012–2013 Scatter Plot (One Month)

Nothing stands out in the three scatter plots. Oklahoma State University versus the University of Oklahoma Health Sciences Center has the tightest cluster of data points around the line of best fit, which is to be expected given the strong correlation. There are no outliers that appear to be exceptional.

The next line graph in **figure 7-27** reduces the time interval to two weeks. Look at the dips in the curves and notice how they line up across the three curves. The peaks line up in a similar fashion. This pattern, which was not apparent with the one-month time interval, appears once the interval is reduced to two weeks. The consistency in the dips and peaks results in higher correlations across the three correlated pairs (see **table 7-2**).

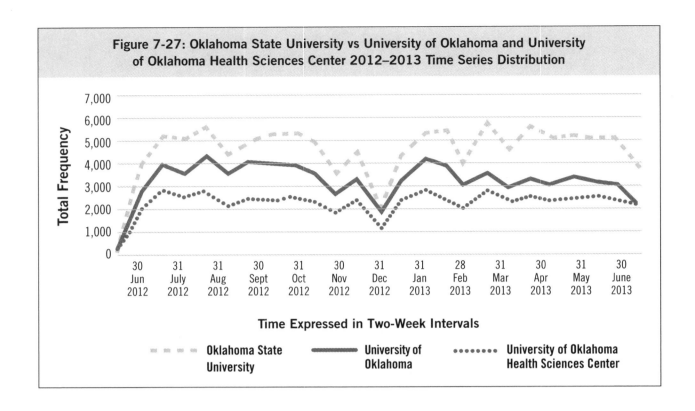

Figure 7-27: Oklahoma State University vs University of Oklahoma and University of Oklahoma Health Sciences Center 2012–2013 Time Series Distribution

Table 7-2: Oklahoma State University vs University of Oklahoma and University of Oklahoma Health Sciences Center 2012–2013 Correlations (Total Frequency over Two-Week Time Interval)	Correlation (r)	Variance in Common (r²)
Oklahoma State University vs University of Oklahoma	0.898	0.806
Oklahoma State University vs University of Oklahoma Health Sciences Center	0.956	0.914
University of Oklahoma vs University of Oklahoma Health Sciences Center	0.897	0.805

With the variance in common between each pair so high (80.5% to 91.4%), the data points will be clustered closely to the line of best fit. It also means that with respect to P-Card expenditures over time, there is a large common element among the three educational institutions (see **figure 7-28**, **figure 7-29**, and **figure 7-30**).

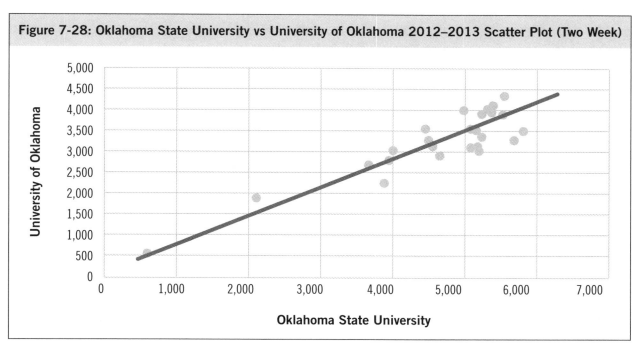

Figure 7-28: Oklahoma State University vs University of Oklahoma 2012–2013 Scatter Plot (Two Week)

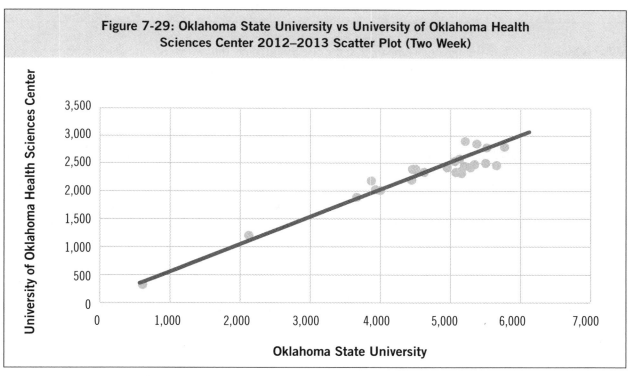

Figure 7-29: Oklahoma State University vs University of Oklahoma Health Sciences Center 2012–2013 Scatter Plot (Two Week)

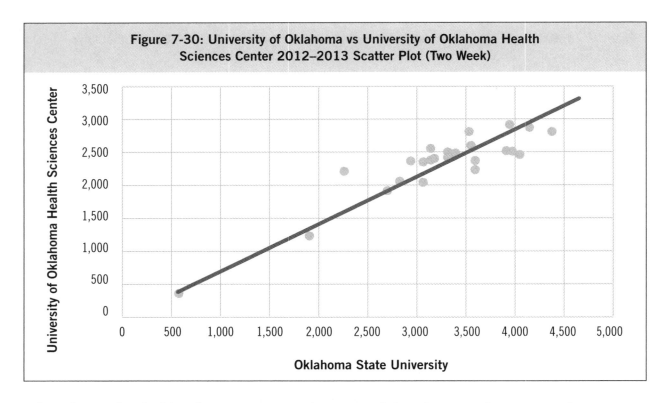

Figure 7-30: University of Oklahoma vs University of Oklahoma Health Sciences Center 2012–2013 Scatter Plot (Two Week)

What is known thus far. Though not as apparent in the one-month data, the two-week time series indicates a strong relationship between the three institutions in 2012–2013 frequency of P-Card transactions. In other words, the shape of the three curves mirrors each other. Note that the frequencies over time are higher for Oklahoma State University, less for the University of Oklahoma, and the University of Oklahoma Health Sciences Center has the lowest frequency.

Validate the External Benchmark: Oklahoma State University (Total Dollar Amount)

Remember there is not a one-to-one correspondence between frequency and dollar value, and as such, more variation is expected. The increase in variation will result in lower correlations and less variance in common. On the plus side, patterns of expenditures can still be seen, and outliers that may seem relatively close on a total frequency distribution may look extremely far away on a total dollar amount distribution. *From a learning perspective, it is worthwhile to observe the different patterns of results, particularly in the scatter plots, that can lead to low correlations and less variance in common.*

Figure 7-31 compares Oklahoma State University to the internal benchmark of the prior year (2011–2012). It appears to track fairly closely. However, upon closer examination, there are points where the rate of increase or decrease is not the same. Consider the data points September to October, October to November, and February to March. The lines connecting these points either move away from each other or toward each other, as opposed to remaining parallel. Consequently, the correlation is weak (.44), with only 19.2% of the variance in common.

The weak relationship is symptomatic of a cluster of data points that form a roughly circular pattern as opposed to a more linear pattern. In the scatter plot in **figure 7-32**, except for a single outlier, the points form a round cluster. As such, it becomes difficult to imagine a single line of best fit through the cluster. Instead, there are multiple possible lines. As the data points become more circular in the cluster, the correlation will approach zero, indicating no relationship between the two variables being compared.

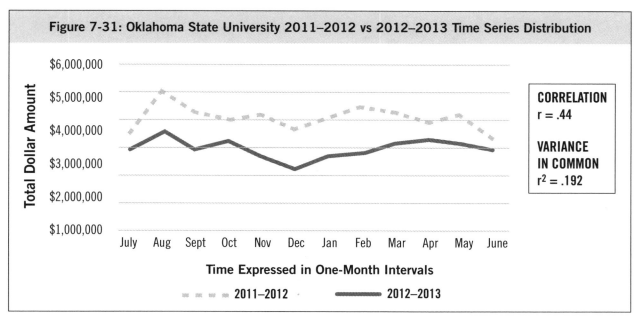

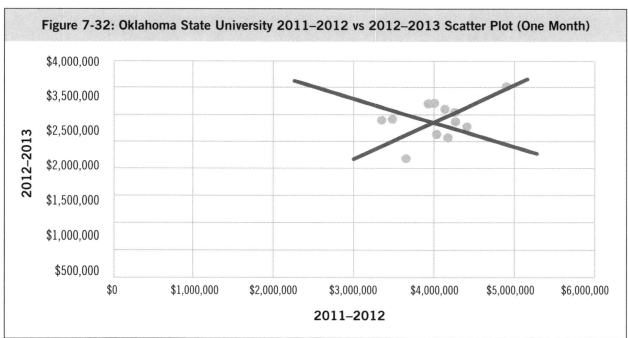

Consider the same data expressed as total frequency over the one-month time interval (**figure 7-11**). From a frequency perspective, the correlation was .837 with a variance in common of .701. The drop in the correlation and variance in common is due to the increased variation in the dollar amounts. The crossed lines in **figure 7-32** represent the fact that a single line of best fit cannot be estimated with an acceptable degree of precision.

Reducing the time interval to two weeks produces a more-jagged curve; however, the relationship between the dips and peaks becomes more pronounced (see **figure 7-33**). The correlation increases to .814 with 66.3% of the variance in common.

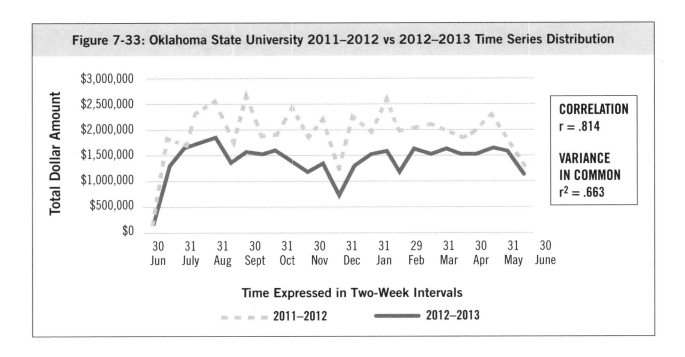

Figure 7-33: Oklahoma State University 2011–2012 vs 2012–2013 Time Series Distribution

The scatter plot in **figure 7-34** becomes more linear as a result. It is an interesting relationship between decreasing the time interval to counterbalance the increased variation in the variables. Of course, if the dips and peaks do not line up, the variance will be further increased. Note that although a .814 correlation seems high, the variance in common is only 66.3%, which is still only moderate.

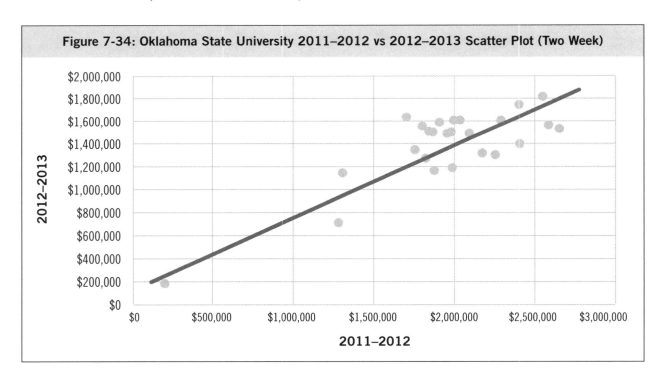

Figure 7-34: Oklahoma State University 2011–2012 vs 2012–2013 Scatter Plot (Two Week)

What is known thus far. With respect to total dollar amount for Oklahoma State University, the relationship is clearer and stronger in the two-week interval data than in the one-month interval data. Notice that the 2012–2013 curve in the two-week data is smoother than for the prior year. This information still supports the use of Oklahoma State University as an external benchmark.

Comparison to the Internal Benchmark, Prior Year (2011–2012): University of Oklahoma and University of Oklahoma Health Sciences Center (Total Dollar Amount)

Thus far, the various line graphs and scatter plots have indicated a variety of relationships, yet the line graphs for the most part have roughly followed each other. **Figure 7-35** is the first example of two line graphs that have a period of time where the data illustrates a very obvious deviation from what is expected. Notice the increase in total dollar amount in February and March 2012–2013 for the University of Oklahoma. **Figure 7-15** illustrates the same time series data from a frequency perspective, which follows a pattern that is expected.

The radical change in the shape of the line for 2012–2013 takes what would likely be a moderate correlation down to a weak correlation, with only 7.2% of the variance in common. On the positive side, an anomaly in the data has been discovered. *Is it known that the controls have been circumvented, compliance to procedures is at fault, or fraud has occurred? No, at this point in the analysis the only thing that is known is that the data is not behaving as expected.*

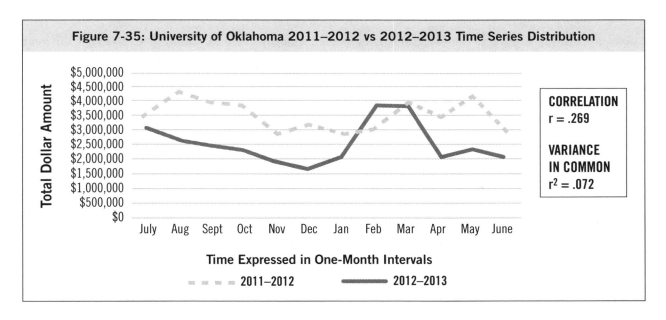

Figure 7-35: University of Oklahoma 2011–2012 vs 2012–2013 Time Series Distribution

The scatter plot in **figure 7-36** illustrates the typical circular cluster of data points indicative of a low correlation. Notice the difficulty in selecting a single line of best fit.

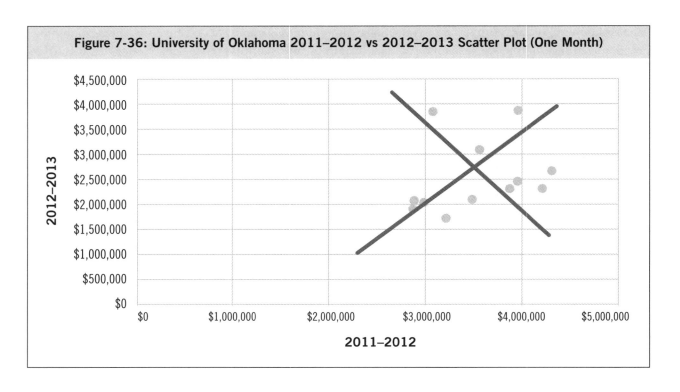

Figure 7-36: University of Oklahoma 2011–2012 vs 2012–2013 Scatter Plot (One Month)

Decreasing the time interval to two weeks illustrates that the anomaly in the data actually occurs in two different time periods (the last two weeks of February and the last two weeks of March). The correlation is still relatively low (.37), as is the variance in common (13.7%). See **figure 7-37**.

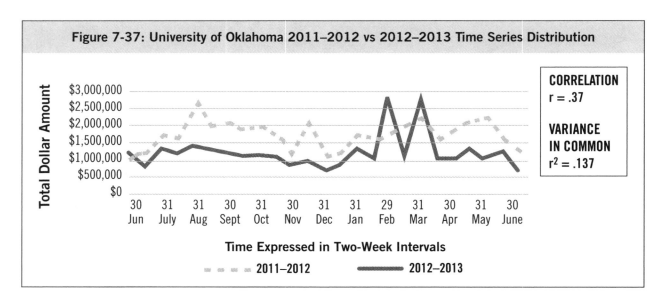

Figure 7-37: University of Oklahoma 2011–2012 vs 2012–2013 Time Series Distribution

The scatter plot in **figure 7-38** does show some linearity with two very prominent outliers (farthest left the last two weeks of February to the right last two weeks of March).

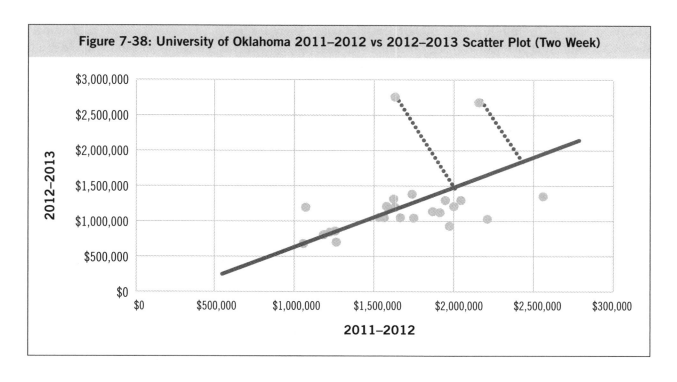

Figure 7-38: University of Oklahoma 2011–2012 vs 2012–2013 Scatter Plot (Two Week)

A second anomaly was discovered in the University of Oklahoma Health Sciences Center in the 2012–2013 data in May (see **figure 7-39**). Though the lines lie relatively close to each other (except for May), the dips and peaks do not line up. This is reflected in a very low correlation of .09 (essentially zero) and a variance in common of less than 1%.

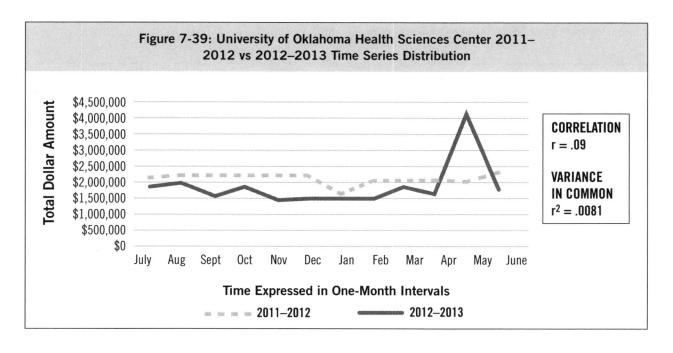

Figure 7-39: University of Oklahoma Health Sciences Center 2011–2012 vs 2012–2013 Time Series Distribution

The scatter plot in **figure 7-40** is interesting because although there is some linearity, the position of the single outlier has enough of an effect to create the roughly circular shape. Note that excluding the outlier would result in a different outcome. However, the purpose of the analysis is to identify the anomalies, not remove them.

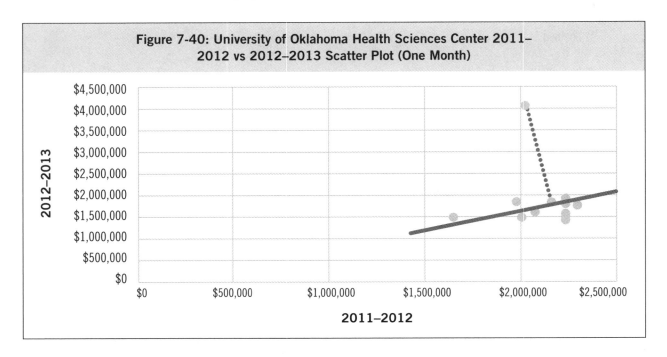

Changing the time interval to the two-week period does alleviate some of the variance. The correlation increases to .485 (weakly moderate) with a variance in common of 23.5%. It is now apparent that the anomaly occurs in the last two weeks of May 2012–2013 (see **figure 7-41**).

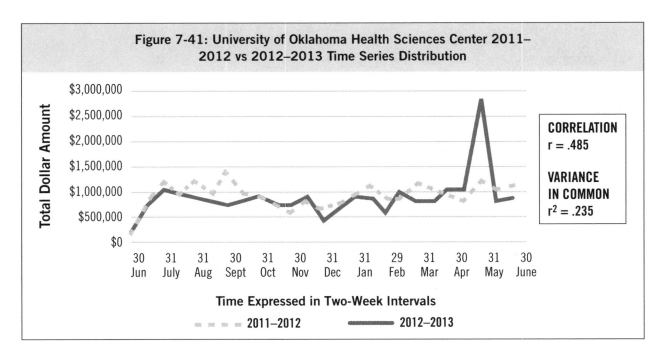

The scatter plot in **figure 7-42** depicts the linearity and the single outlier (with the dropped perpendicular) for the last two weeks of May in 2012–2013.

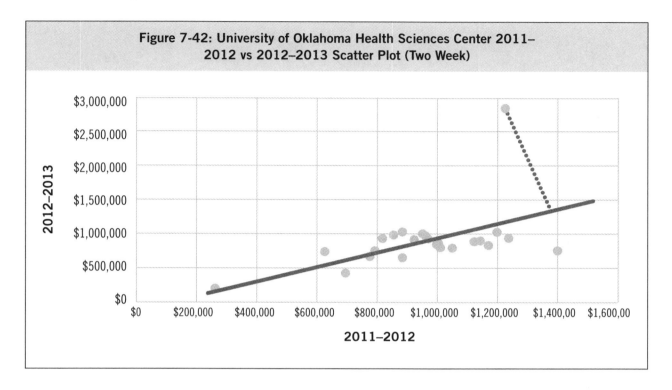

Figure 7-42: University of Oklahoma Health Sciences Center 2011–2012 vs 2012–2013 Scatter Plot (Two Week)

What is known thus far. It is obvious that the strength of the relationships, as indicated by the correlations, have decreased when total dollar value is considered versus total frequency. The single strong correlation with the prior year was found with Oklahoma State University. For the remaining two institutions, linearity does exist, but the presence of outliers served to distort the correlations. The outliers for the University of Oklahoma were in the last two weeks of February and the last two weeks of March 2012–2013. For the University of Oklahoma Health Sciences Center, the outlier was in the last two weeks of May 2012–2013.

Comparison to the External Benchmark: Oklahoma State University (Total Dollar Amount)

In 2012–2013, there are two marked differences between the line representing the external benchmark (Oklahoma State University) and the lines for the remaining two institutions (the University of Oklahoma and the University of Oklahoma Health Sciences Center). Both of the anomalies were identified previously in comparison to the internal benchmark. Seeing both anomalies again relative to the external benchmark further solidifies that these time periods are not behaving as expected (see **figure 7-43**).

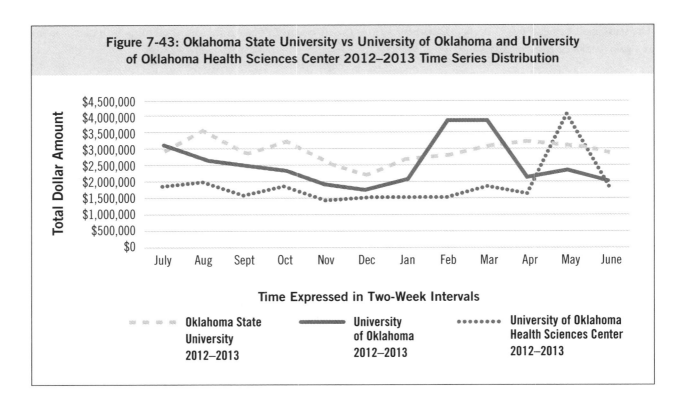

Figure 7-43: Oklahoma State University vs University of Oklahoma and University of Oklahoma Health Sciences Center 2012–2013 Time Series Distribution

The weak correlations are indicative of the impact of the anomalies on the comparison of the relationship among the various pairs of institutions. Understandably, the variance in common is also very low (see **table 7-3**).

Table 7-3: Oklahoma State University vs University of Oklahoma and University of Oklahoma Health Sciences Center 2012–2013 Correlations (Total Dollar Amount over One-Month Time Interval)	Correlation (r)	Variance in Common (r²)
Oklahoma State University vs University of Oklahoma	0.286	.082
Oklahoma State University vs University of Oklahoma Health Sciences Center	0.351	.123
University of Oklahoma vs University of Oklahoma Health Sciences Center	-0.004	0

The scatter plots support the correlations. The three scatter plots in **figure 7-44**, **figure 7-45**, and **figure 7-46** have similar shapes. There is some linearity, yet the linearity is offset by the one or two outliers. Those outliers correspond to the anomalies that have been identified.

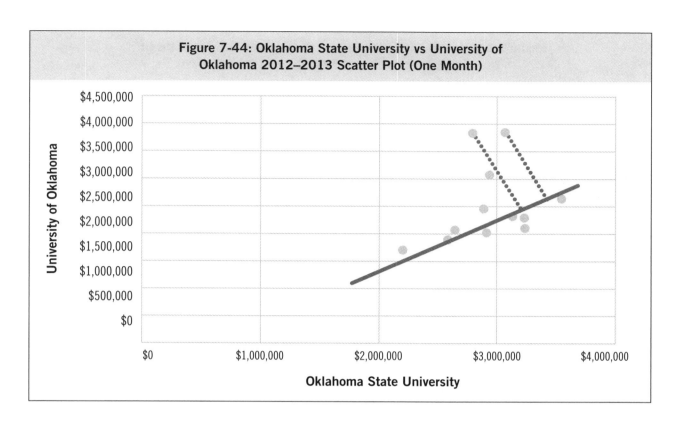

Figure 7-44: Oklahoma State University vs University of Oklahoma 2012–2013 Scatter Plot (One Month)

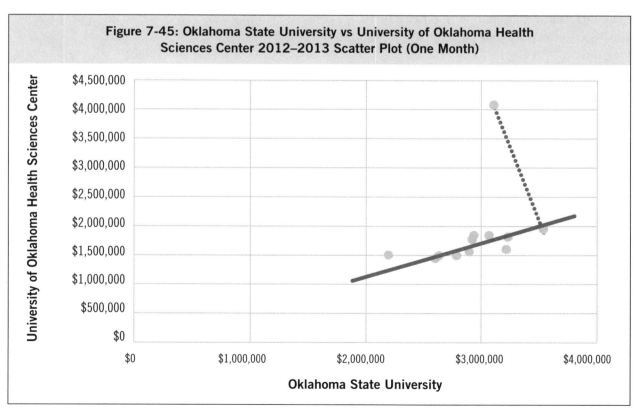

Figure 7-45: Oklahoma State University vs University of Oklahoma Health Sciences Center 2012–2013 Scatter Plot (One Month)

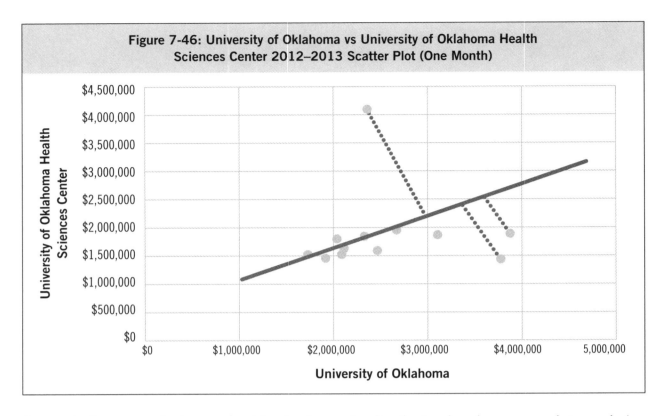

Figure 7-46: University of Oklahoma vs University of Oklahoma Health Sciences Center 2012–2013 Scatter Plot (One Month)

A very similar pattern is demonstrated in the time series distribution based on two-week intervals (see **figure 7-47**, **table 7-4**, **figure 7-48**, and **figure 7-49**). The correlations and variance in common are again fairly low. The three scatter plots indicate some linearity and the outliers corresponding to the anomalies.

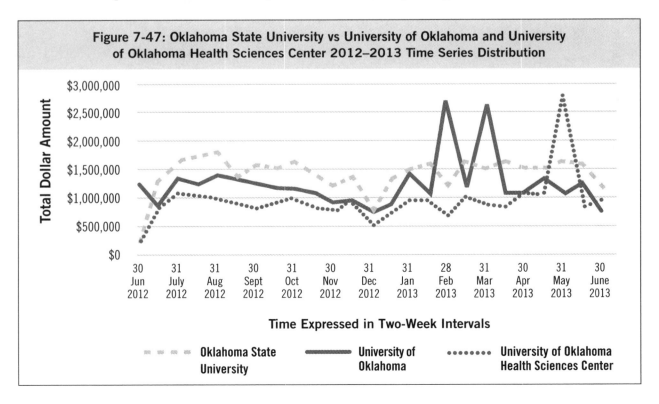

Figure 7-47: Oklahoma State University vs University of Oklahoma and University of Oklahoma Health Sciences Center 2012–2013 Time Series Distribution

Table 7-4: Oklahoma State University vs University of Oklahoma and University of Oklahoma Health Sciences Center 2012–2013 Correlations (Total Dollar Amount over Two-Week Time Interval)	Correlation (r)	Variance in Common (r²)
Oklahoma State University vs University of Oklahoma	0.108	0.012
Oklahoma State University vs University of Oklahoma Health Sciences Center	0.483	0.233
University of Oklahoma vs University of Oklahoma Health Sciences Center	-0.067	0.004

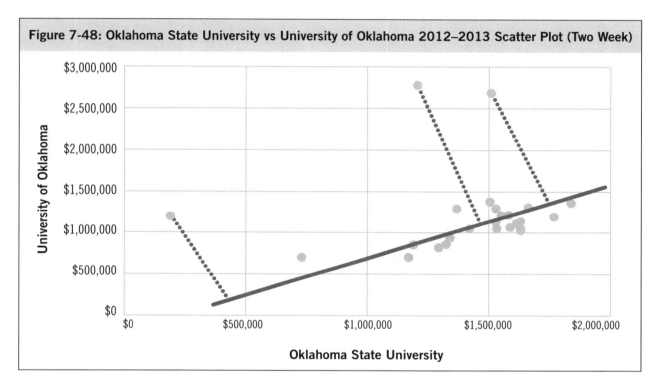

Figure 7-48: Oklahoma State University vs University of Oklahoma 2012–2013 Scatter Plot (Two Week)

Note that there are three outliers rather than the expected two. The outlier farthest to the left in the graph represents the last two weeks of June 2012. In **figure 7-47**, it can be seen that the data for the University of Oklahoma trends up during this period while the other two institutions trend down.

Note that the scatter plot in **figure 7-50** illustrates all four of the identified outliers.

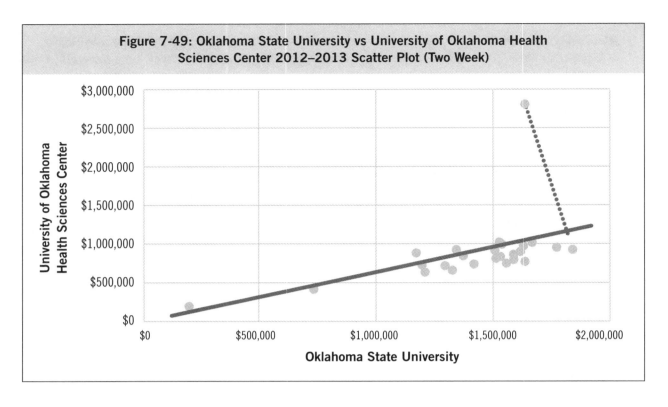

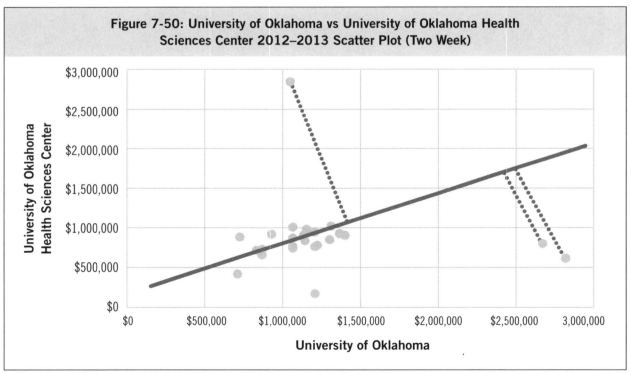

What is known thus far. The relationship discovered when the 2012–2013 data was compared to the internal benchmark (prior year 2011–2012) was supported in the comparison with the external benchmark. In addition, the last two weeks of June 2012 for the University of Oklahoma was identified as another outlier.

Summary – What's Important

- Always validate the benchmark so that what is normal can be separated from the unusual.

- Particularly when two curves lie very close to each other, the only way to check the strength of the apparent relationship is to calculate the correlation.

- Time series analysis can be performed using either total frequency or total dollar amount. Total frequency has less variability associated with it, resulting in the curve being less jagged.

- Total dollar amount has more variability associated with it, which will be reflected in the curve.

- Unusual dollar amounts that will not be apparent in the total frequency curve will appear in the total dollar amount curve.

- r^2 discriminates between strong and weak relationships to a greater extent than the correlation.

Chapter 8

CASE STUDY: COMPARISON OF THE FREQUENCY ANALYSIS RESULTS TO THE TIME SERIES ANALYSIS RESULTS

Different Perspectives—Are They Consistent?

Though the frequency analysis and the time series analysis provide different perspectives on the data, the results of each analytical procedure should be compared to each other. In some cases, the results of the two procedures will support each other. In other cases, they will highlight different findings. It is important to note where they confirm a certain finding and where there are unique findings.

Table 8-1 lists the 14 transactions that are greater than $60,000 and their transaction dates. It can be seen that the three largest transactions fall within the three time periods that were identified in the time series analysis—the last two weeks of February and March 2013 for the University of Oklahoma and the last two weeks of May 2013 for the University of Oklahoma Health Sciences Center.

Table 8-1: Comparison of the Transactions Greater than $60,000 with Their Transaction Dates		
University Name	**Dollar Amount**	**Date of Transaction**
University of Oklahoma	$1,764,140.27	20-Feb-2013
University of Oklahoma Health Sciences Center	$1,760,390.90	21-May-2013
University of Oklahoma	$1,603,377.85	20-Mar-2013
University of Oklahoma	$877,026.12	30-Jun-2012
University of Oklahoma Health Sciences Center	$191,419.82	19-Apr-2013
University of Oklahoma	$102,805.90	08-Aug-2012
University of Oklahoma Health Sciences Center	$102,005.73	19-Jun-2013
University of Oklahoma	$95,400.00	08-Sep-2012
University of Oklahoma Health Sciences Center	$92,161.56	06-Dec-2012
University of Oklahoma Health Sciences Center	$86,745.00	13-May-2013
University of Oklahoma	$78,098.48	30-Jul-2012
University of Oklahoma Health Sciences Center	$77,000.00	13-Feb-2013
University of Oklahoma Health Sciences Center	$71,475.74	16-Apr-2013
University of Oklahoma	$63,008.00	29-Jun-2012

Looking at the total dollar amount for each of the three intervals in **table 8-2**, it can be seen that the three largest transactions could account for the swing in the total dollar amounts from below the benchmark value to well above the benchmark value.

Table 8-2: Total Dollar Amount by Two-Week Interval		
University Name	**Two-Week Date Interval**	**Total Dollar Amount**
University of Oklahoma	Feb 16 to Feb 28, 2013	$1,202,500.02
University of Oklahoma	March 16 to March 31, 2013	$1,506,363.06
University of Oklahoma Health Sciences Center	May 16 to May 31, 2013	$2,848,909.54

Removing the three largest transactions from the data set produces the following time series graphs and their respective correlations. Note the difference in the curves compared to **figure 7-43** and **figure 7-47**. As a result, the correlations have changed yet the relationships described previously are still apparent. In the one-month data, there is a stronger relationship between the external benchmark (Oklahoma State University) and the University of Oklahoma Health Sciences Center than with the University of Oklahoma (see **figure 8-1** and **table 8-3**).

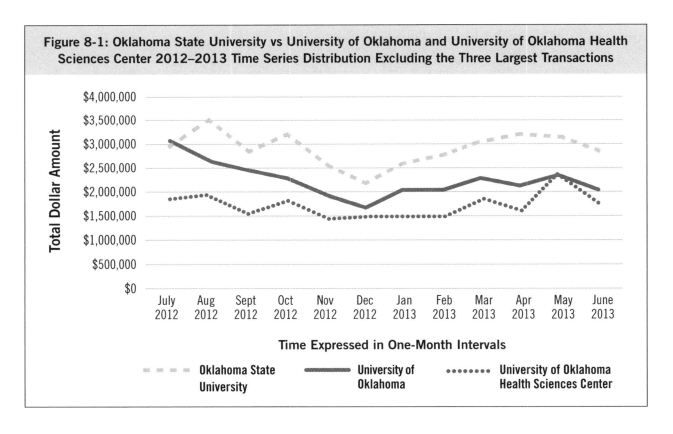

Figure 8-1: Oklahoma State University vs University of Oklahoma and University of Oklahoma Health Sciences Center 2012–2013 Time Series Distribution Excluding the Three Largest Transactions

Table 8-3: Oklahoma State University vs University of Oklahoma and University of Oklahoma Health Sciences Center 2012–2013 Correlations (Total Dollar Amount over One-Month Time Interval) Excluding the Three Largest Transactions		
	Correlation (r)	Variance in Common (r^2)
Oklahoma State University vs University of Oklahoma	.585	.342
Oklahoma State University vs University of Oklahoma Health Sciences Center	.638	.407
University of Oklahoma vs University of Oklahoma Health Sciences Center	.508	.258

When the time interval is reduced to a two-week interval, the relationship becomes even more accentuated with the correlation between Oklahoma State University and the University of Oklahoma Health Sciences Center, reaching .867 with a variance in common of 75.2% (see **figure 8-2** and **table 8-4**). This relationship is not apparent in **figure 7-43**, and the correlations in **table 7-3** are significantly impacted by the presence of the outliers.

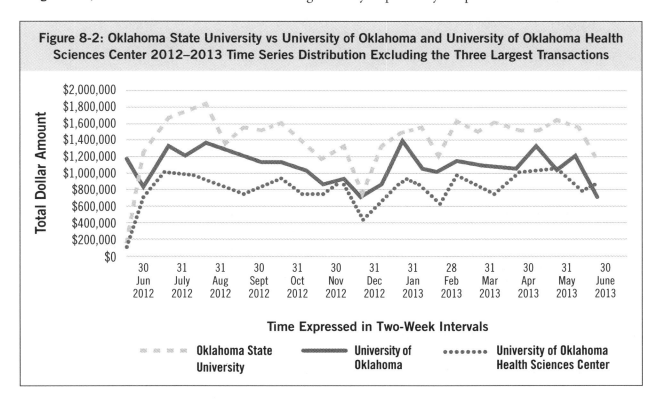

Figure 8-2: Oklahoma State University vs University of Oklahoma and University of Oklahoma Health Sciences Center 2012–2013 Time Series Distribution Excluding the Three Largest Transactions

Table 8-4: Oklahoma State University vs University of Oklahoma and University of Oklahoma Health Sciences Center 2012–2013 Correlations (Total Dollar Amount over Two-Week Time Interval) Excluding the Three Largest Transactions		
	Correlation (r)	Variance in Common (r^2)
Oklahoma State University vs University of Oklahoma	.408	.166
Oklahoma State University vs University of Oklahoma Health Sciences Center	.867	.752
University of Oklahoma vs University of Oklahoma Health Sciences Center	.323	.104

Interestingly, the most significant outlier in the University of Oklahoma, once the three largest transactions have been removed, are the transactions that had transaction dates in the last two weeks of June 2012 (see **figure 8-3**). This group of transactions can be seen in **figure 7-48**, but it was overshadowed by the other two outliers.

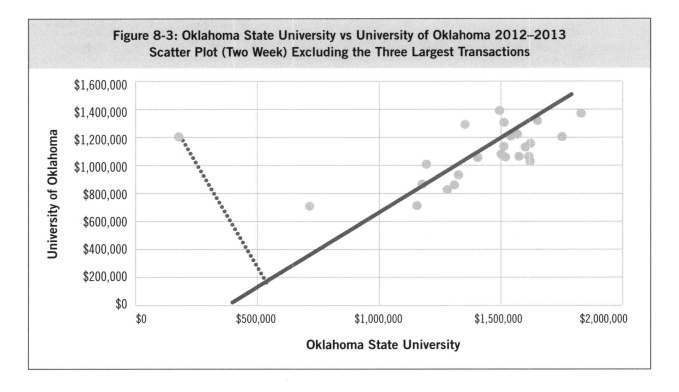

Figure 8-3: Oklahoma State University vs University of Oklahoma 2012–2013 Scatter Plot (Two Week) Excluding the Three Largest Transactions

What is known thus far. The results from the frequency analysis are consistent with the results of the time series analysis. Both point to the three largest dollar value transactions. Note that this does not reduce the risk to the remaining transactions that exceed $10,000. Removal of the three largest dollar value transactions indicates an additional subset of transactions may be considered high risk—those being the transactions with a transaction date in the last two weeks of June 2012.

Outcomes from the Analytical Procedures

The following subsets were identified as not behaving as expected in the 2012–2013 data. From the frequency analysis:

- University of Oklahoma: 188 transactions greater than $10,000 and less than $60,000 with a total dollar value of $3,880,965.20

- University of Oklahoma Health Sciences Center: 117 transactions greater than $10,000 and less than $60,000 with a total dollar value of $2,546,358.34

- University of Oklahoma: 7 transactions greater than $60,000 with a total dollar value of $4,583,856.62

- University of Oklahoma Health Sciences Center: 7 transactions greater than $60,000 with a total dollar value of $2,381,198.75

From the time series analysis:

- University of Oklahoma: 584 transactions with a total dollar value of $1,205,302.91 with transaction dates occurring in the last two weeks of June 2012

Mutually Exclusive Subsets

Before the subsets can be placed into a sample frame for consideration of different selection strategies, care must be taken to ensure that the subsets are mutually exclusive. In other words, transactions in the high-risk subsets that occur as a result of the frequency analysis cannot also be contained in the high-risk subsets resulting from the time series analysis. This determination cannot be done until the high-risk subsets from both analytical procedures have been identified.

In this case, the 584 transactions that occurred in the last two weeks for the University of Oklahoma were isolated and then sorted into a frequency distribution using a frequency interval of $10,000. The transactions in the two categories greater than $10,000 and less than $60,000 and greater than $60,000 were identified (see **table 8-5**).

	Last Two Weeks of June 2012		Frequency Analysis	
Table 8-5: University of Oklahoma Transactions in Common Between Frequency Analysis and Time Series Analysis	**Total Dollar Amount**	**Total Frequency**	**Total Dollar Amount**	**Total Frequency**
Greater than $10,000 and less than $60,000	$148,995.47	7	$3,880,965.20	188
Greater than $60,000	$940,034.12	2	$4,583,856.62	7

For simplicity's sake, it was decided to remove the nine transactions that were identified as being in high-risk subsets for analyses from the last two weeks June 2012 subset (time series) and maintain them with the associated subsets from the frequency analysis. This would mean that the time series high-risk subset must be altered to reflect the removal of the nine in common transactions, resulting in 575 transactions with a total dollar value of $116,273.32 having transaction dates occurring in the last two weeks of June 2012 for the University of Oklahoma.

Given the new dollar value, the auditor needs to consider whether this subset should still remain as high risk. The dollar value is substantially lower; however, these transactions had transaction dates prior to July 1, 2012. A total of 99.5% of the transactions prior to July 1 occurred in the last week of June, with 14% of them occurring on Saturday, June 30, 2012. For the sake of this example, consider this to be unusual and thus the subset will remain a high-risk subset. The high-risk subsets are summarized in **table 8-6**.

Table 8-6: University of Oklahoma and University of Oklahoma Health Sciences Center 2012–2013 High-Risk Subsets vs Total Population		
	University of Oklahoma	University of Oklahoma Health Sciences Center
Total Number of High-Risk Transactions	770	124
Total Dollar Amount from High-Risk Transactions	$8,581,095.13	$4,927,557.09
Total Number of Transactions in Population	81,711	57,942
Total Dollar Amount in Population	$30,527,905.31	$22,603,378.77

The analytical procedures reduced the 81,711 transactions down to 770, which accounted for roughly 28% of the University of Oklahoma's total P-Card expenditures. For the University of Oklahoma Health Sciences Center, 124 high-risk transactions were identified, which corresponded to roughly 22% of their total P-Card expenditures.

The next section deals with the selection strategies for the high-risk subsets. However, the question still remains: what to do with the transactions that, based on the analytical procedures, are not considered high risk? Ignoring the low- and medium-risk transactions would necessitate a change in the scope of the audit. Changing scope, though a possible solution, is likely not the preferred solution. It is unlikely that most audit teams would have sufficient sample size (and resources) to examine anything beyond the already-identified high-risk subsets. Consequently auditors should consider other evidence collection methods such as observation, inquiry, confirmation, inspection, recalculation, and re-performance as viable alternatives to examine the low- and medium-risk subsets.

Summary – What's Important

- Always compare the results of the frequency analysis to the results of the time series analysis. Ensure that the items in common to the high-risk subsets from both analyses are identified.

- Adjust the final results so that subsets are mutually exclusive.

SELECTING ITEMS FOR TESTING TO OBTAIN AUDIT EVIDENCE

Chapter 9

SELECTING ITEMS FOR TESTING

There are three methods of selecting items for testing. Selecting all items and selecting specific items do not use randomness (such as a random number generator) to select items, whereas random sampling (sometimes called audit sampling) does use a random number generator to select items.

Selecting All Items

The possibility of examining all transactions in a specific subset is based on one of two conditions being met: a) the number of transactions or items in the subset is small enough that the auditor can examine all transactions or items; or b) sufficient data is in an electronic format and technology (such as ACL or IDEA) is available to examine all transactions or items regardless of the number of transactions or items.

Selecting all items implies that a complete subset has been chosen for examination. The assumption underlying the creation of the subsets is that the only distinguishing characteristic between this subset and any other subset is that it has been identified as high risk. To be more specific, selecting all items does not apply to subsets that contain only those items that are deemed to be suspicious or problematic, such as being fraudulent (selecting specific items).

It should be noted that the selection of suspicious or fraudulent items, which will be considered in the following section, is not technically a part of analytical procedures. Selecting all items and selecting specific items follow two very distinct procedures. Selecting fraudulent items results from the use of fraud red flags, scanning items by the auditor, and the use of generic or customized scripts found in ACL or IDEA. The selection is performed at the transaction level. The identification of high-risk subsets (selecting all items) results from the integration of the risk assessment with the subdivision of the data set. The selection in this instance is done at the subset level. Note that the distinction between selecting all items and selecting specific items rests on the need to separate the selection of specific items from the remaining subsets due to the uniqueness of the selection criteria (such as fraud red flags).

If there is a sufficient amount of the data available in an electronic format to evaluate effectiveness of controls or compliance to procedures, or at the very least, identify which items or transactions contravene either a control or a procedure, then the use of technology is an efficient way to examine large numbers of transactions and isolate the exceptions. However, if the outcome of the application of technology results in another large data set in which the transactions cannot be definitively determined to be problematic, the advantage of using technology has been greatly diminished.

Case Study

Consider the frequency and time series analyses performed on the University of Oklahoma and the University of Oklahoma Health Sciences Center 2012–2013 P-Card expenditures. Five subsets were identified as being high risk based on the analytical procedures. In an actual audit, the selection of these subsets would have been validated with appropriate management.

Table 9-1: High-Risk Subsets Identified from the Frequency and Time Series Analyses		
2012–2013 P-Card Expenditures	University of Oklahoma	University of Oklahoma Health Sciences Center
Greater than $10,000 and less than $60,000	N = 188 Total Dollar Value = $3,880,965.20	N = 117 Total Dollar Value = $2,546,358.34
Greater than $60,000	N = 7 Total Dollar Value = $4,583,856.62	N = 7 Total Dollar Value = $2,381,198.75
Last two weeks of June 2012	N = 575 Total Dollar Value = $116,273.32	

Note that the sample frame illustrated in **table 9-1** is not balanced. In other words, there are three cells for the University of Oklahoma and two cells for the University of Oklahoma Health Sciences Center. This is as it should be, though some may be uncomfortable with an unbalanced design.

If all of the relevant information is in an electronic format and the technology is available, all of the subsets could be examined in their entirety. In fact, all of the 2012–2013 transactions for the University of Oklahoma and the University of Oklahoma Health Sciences Center could be examined in this manner. The analytical procedures would not be necessary because reduction of the data set based on risk would no longer be required.

Select all items also applies to the condition in which analytical procedures were applied, and some of the subsets were small enough to allow them to be examined in their entirety. In **table 9-1**, the two subsets containing transactions greater than $60,000 would be examined in their entirety. Because randomization was not used in the selection of these items, generalization and extrapolation beyond the defined subsets cannot be performed. Nor can these items be subjected to statistical tests.

Selecting Specific Items

Throughout the audit, the auditor will be creating a subset containing items or transactions that are suspicious, unusual, or potentially fraudulent. This subset is *not* considered an outcome of analytical procedures, yet it is a valid and very important subset.

The selection criteria for selecting specific items underscores the belief of the auditor that the transactions or items are in some way problematic, which will become clear upon closer examination. Since the transactions or items are selected because they are potentially invalid, it stands to reason, particularly if the auditor in question is proficient at selecting such transactions or items, that a calculated error rate would likely be extremely high. For this reason, error rates are not reported for this type of evidence, though the selection criteria and the results of the examination of the transactions are described in detail.

Because randomization was not used in the selection of these items, generalization and extrapolation beyond the defined subsets cannot be performed. Nor can these items be subjected to statistical tests.

The use of criteria such as fraud red flags allows the auditor to target specific transactions or items rather than large groups of items that are identified by the analytical procedures. There are a variety of fraud red flags available on the internet and in articles by various experts in the field. Auditors should be aware that some of the fraud red flags are generic and would apply to most processes in a business entity. However, there are always red flags that are unique to any specific industry.

Both ACL and IDEA have generic scripts that can be used to identify transactions meeting the more common red flags. Both software programs allow auditors to create customized scripts that can be tailored to more specific red flags that may be unique to certain industries.

Maintaining Credibility

Many clients become uncomfortable when transactions are selected without using a random number generator. Part of the auditor's responsibility is to educate clients about selecting transactions (either selecting all items or selecting specific items). Both types of evidence depend on the use of specific criteria to identify groups of transactions or specific individual transactions. The auditor should be totally transparent with the client about the criteria being used.

Regardless of the nature of the criteria, all criteria should be documented in the working papers and disclosed in the audit report. These criteria should be defensible and able to withstand scrutiny. Fraud red flags, particularly those that are unique to a given industry or have had a history of occurrence within the business entity, should be embedded in the audit procedures, thus becoming a permanent part of the performance of every audit.

Case Study

The results from the analytical procedures that were applied to the University of Oklahoma and the University of Oklahoma Health Sciences Center have been extended to include two subsets containing potentially fraudulent transactions (see **table 9-2**). Note that these two subsets are fabricated data and included at this point purely for the purpose of illustration.

Table 9-2: High-Risk Subsets Identified from the Frequency and Time Series Analyses with Two Fraud Subsets		
2012–2013 P-Card Expenditures	**University of Oklahoma**	**University of Oklahoma Health Sciences Center**
Greater than $10,000 and less than $60,000	N = 188 Total Dollar Value = $3,880,965.20	N = 117 Total Dollar Value = $2,546,358.34
Greater than $60,000	N = 7 Total Dollar Value = $4,583,856.62	N = 7 Total Dollar Value = $2,381,198.75
Last two weeks of June 2012	N = 575 Total Dollar Value = $116,273.32	
Fraud red flags (added as an example)	N = 10 Total Dollar Value = $10,145.00	N = 6 Total Dollar Value = $5,200.00

The sample frame shown above now contains two subsets that represent select all items (transactions greater than $60,000) and two subsets that represent select specific items (fraud red flags).

Random Sampling

Random sampling is appropriate when the number of transactions in a given subset is too large to look at all of them and the auditor wishes to form an opinion about the subset in its entirety.

The Randomness Assumption

The randomness assumption is composed of two parts. Every item in the population or subset from which the random sample is being drawn must have an equal probability of being selected. The auditor must ensure that this assumption is met by checking to see that each item has a unique identifier. In an electronic data set, the simplest unique identifier is the row number. If an arbitrarily imposed numbering system such as a client number, invoice number, check number, employee number, or case number is used, the auditor must ensure that the numbering of the items is sequential with no gaps.

The second part of the randomness assumption states that the selection of a single item must not affect the probability of selection of another item. This is seldom a problem with an electronic data set because the selection of individual transactions is done electronically. However, if the selection is done manually, as in haphazard selection, the selected subset will not be random and will be biased. In the selection of physical commodities, human nature will always play a role. Items that are difficult to reach (such as those on a high self or the bottom of a pile) will be ignored in favor of selecting the more accessible items. To counter this tendency, all items in the population or subset from which the random sample is to be drawn should be numbered and a random number generator used to identify which items are to be selected.

The ultimate objective of performing a random sample is to be able to generalize the findings of the random sample to the population from which it was drawn. If the randomness assumptions are not met, then the selected sample is biased, as is any subsequent generalization.

Variations on Random Selection

Random selection of the item is considered the norm in applied research. In this scenario, every item (or transaction) has an equal probability of being selected and the items are selected as a single batch by a random number generator. A variation on this method, which also selects the item or transaction, is *sequential* or *systematic random sampling*. In this method, the auditor randomly selects a start point, typically called a seed value, and then adds a constant skip interval to the seed value, such as every 50th item.

In this case, the auditor would randomly select a start point using a random number generator (i.e., selecting a sample size of 1 from a range of possible numbers—depending on the size of the data set; use a range that does not result in the exclusion of a large portion of the population if the upper limit is selected as the seed value). Note that using a random number generator is critical if the randomness assumption is to be met. If a random generator is not used to select the start point, this method slips into haphazard sampling. Sequential or systematic random sampling is most commonly used when the auditor or researcher wishes to ensure that the full range of values in the population has been covered.

However, auditors (particularly external auditors) are faced with the challenge that some items such as those with high-dollar values have an inherently higher risk than other items. *Dollar unit* or *monetary unit sampling* was designed to address this situation. It has an inherent bias (when compared to the norm of randomly selecting the transaction) that results in a larger number of high-dollar value transactions being selected than low-dollar transactions. Rather than using the transaction as the sampling unit, the dollar is randomly chosen. Because high-dollar transactions have more dollars associated with them, they have a greater probability of selection than low-dollar value transactions. **Table 9-3** illustrates the comparison in randomly selecting the transaction versus randomly selecting the dollar.

Table 9-3: Comparison of a Simple Random Sample to a Dollar Unit Sample			
Dollar Value of Transactions	**Frequency of Transactions**	**Simple Random Sample (n=35)**	**Dollar Unit Sample (n=35)**
High-Dollar Value	X X X X X X X X X X X X X X X X X X X X X X X X	X X X X	X X X X X X X X X X X X X X X X X X X
Medium-Dollar Value	X X X X X X X X X X X X X X X X X X X X X X X X X X X X X X X X X X X X X	X X X X X X X X X X	X X X X X X X X X
Low-Dollar Value	X X X X X X X X X X X X X X X X X X X X X X X X X X X X X X X X X X X X X X X X X X X X X X X X X X X X X X X X X X X	X X X X X X X X X X X X X X X X XX X X X X X X X X X X X X X X X X	X X X X X

Note that a simple random sample would contain very few high-dollar value transactions, while the reverse would be true for a dollar unit sample. The low-dollar value transactions, more frequent in number, would occupy a greater proportion of the simple random sample and a smaller proportion in the dollar unit sample.

A random sample depends on the use of a random number generator or, at the very least, random number tables that have been generated using a random number algorithm. There are many ways in which a random sample can be drawn. Computer assisted audit techniques (CAATs), particularly ACL and IDEA have random number generators, as does Excel. There are also random number generators available online.

Dollar unit sampling uses sequential random sampling (randomly selected start point, constant skip interval) to select transactions for the random sample. The benefit of dollar unit sampling (selecting proportionally higher-dollar value transactions than low-dollar transactions) rests on there being a relatively large distance between the lowest-dollar value and the highest-dollar value transaction. With the increasing use of subdivision to identify the critical few high-risk subsets in very large data sets, the effective distance between the lowest- and highest-dollar value transactions has been greatly reduced, resulting in transactions within the same subset having roughly the same dollar value and therefore the same probability of selection. Though dollar unit sampling can still be performed in these situations, it is simpler to draw a simple random sample.

Regardless of the random number generator being employed, proof that a random sample was drawn must be included in the working papers. In this instance, proof means a screen shot of the input into the random generator and a screen shot of the output from the random number generator.

Haphazard Sampling

Hall (2013) defines a haphazard sampling as follows: "Haphazard sampling is a non-statistical technique used by auditors to simulate random sampling when testing the error status of accounting populations." Research from a series of articles authored by Hall and his colleagues from 2000 to 2013 clearly demonstrates that haphazard sampling is biased. No matter how hard an auditor tries to replicate a random sample, the haphazard sample more often than not will be biased. The critical difference between drawing a haphazard sample and drawing a random sample is that there is no human intervention in the selection of random transactions. Human interference in haphazard selection, whether consciously or unconsciously, results in certain transactions being selected with a greater frequency than other transactions. As a result, this directly contravenes the equal probability assumption that is critical to randomness.

Unfortunately haphazard sampling is still frequently used, typically under the misconception that it is easier to perform than random sampling. It cannot be stressed enough that biased selection results in biased results being generalized onto the population.

Selecting Items from Physical Commodities

Selecting items for examination from an electronic data set is relatively straightforward. ACL and IDEA both have random number algorithms that can randomly select items from large data sets. If they are not available, Excel and Random.org can create random samples that the auditor can then remove from the electronic population for examination.

Selecting items from physical commodities is not nearly so straightforward. Physical commodities seldom have unique identifiers attached to them, thus requiring the auditor to number all items. The physical layout of the items does not lend itself to random selection by the auditor. The largest challenge is time—in many industries, items do not sit around for an extended period of time. Industries that have large transportation fleets, assembly lines, retail outlets, or perishable goods have items that are constantly on the move.

The challenge in the field is how much is known in advance and how much will be discovered once the auditor arrives on site. If possible, the following should be identified in advance of the on-site visit:

1. For selection of specific items, identify the critical characteristics that constitute a potentially problematic item. If the items are known in advance, such as specific vehicles in a fleet of vehicles with a specific accident or maintenance history, list those items in advance. If possible, determine if they might be on site when the auditor is selecting items.

2. Find out the physical layout of the site at which the items are located. If the site is very large, consider the possibility of dividing the site into several quadrants and then randomly selecting the quadrants before randomly selecting items within a quadrant.

3. Find out what reports are available from site management that will identify the size of the population available, the locations of specific items, and how fast the items move through the facility. The latter is specifically relevant to transportation fleets, which may only be in a specific facility for maintenance or loading or unloading goods.

4. Know how many resources will be available to conduct the selection and how long it takes to examine individual items.

The following steps should be performed for random selection:

1. Bound the population. Identify all of the items from which the random sample will be drawn. Note that the physical location impacts how the population is bounded. If the items are spread over several locations within the same facility, multiple populations will be bounded and therefore the sample size must be spread across the various populations. When items are spread over a large geographical area, subdivide the area into roughly equal quadrants. Randomly select the quadrants to be examined.

2. For each population (or quadrant), count the number of items that make up the population.

3. Establish a numbering system that ensures all items within the population (or quadrant) are numbered.

4. Use Random.org to identify the random sample.

5. Select the items that were identified in the Random.org sample.

From a sampling perspective, the greatest challenge facing auditors is the risk of selection bias. Human beings frequently take the path of least resistance. For example, given a choice between climbing up on a foot stool to reach a retail item placed on an upper shelf versus selecting an identical retail item from a lower shelf, chances are that the individual will select the item that is within reach. The same is true in facilities that cover a large area. More sampling is performed in the areas close by than in the areas farther away. The result of this type of selection is that selection of items within easy reach impacts the probability of selection of items farther away. Thus the independence assumption of randomness has been compromised and the sample can no longer be deemed random and is considered to be biased.

Evidence of how the random selection was performed in terms of screen shots of the input and output must be placed in the working papers. For future reference, how the physical area was subdivided to form smaller subpopulations and how the items in the population were numbered should be recorded in the working papers. This will provide future auditors with a starting point, rather than starting from scratch.

Summary – What's Important

Selecting All Items

- Selecting all items was originally envisioned to accommodate the situation when technology was available to analyse complete data sets. In this instance, analytical procedures would not be needed, nor would the various item selection strategies.

- Selecting all items also applies to subsets that are small enough that the auditor can examine all items in the subset. In this instance, the subset to be examined was created through subdivision based on the risk assessment.

- The results from selecting all items cannot be generalized or extrapolated to other subsets, nor can this data be subjected to statistical tests.

Selecting Specific Items

- Selecting specific items results based on the use of fraud red flags and the auditor's knowledge and experience in identifying unusual transactions.

- It is different from selecting all items in that the composition of the subset is made up of items that are believed to be suspicious or problematic.

- Random sampling was not employed and therefore the results cannot be generalized, extrapolated, or subjected to statistical tests.

- Auditors should document the criteria used to subdivide data sets and the criteria used to select unusual transactions.

Random Sampling

- The easiest way to meet the randomness assumption is to use a random number generator. However, randomly selecting physical commodities is always subject to human nature. As such, the auditor must ensure that the assumption of independence is met.

Sampling Physical Commodities

- Clearly define the subsets that contain select specific items and select all items.

- Bound the population, taking into account the spread of the items over geographic areas.

- Establish a numbering system and select the random sample.

- Be aware of human nature to select the most easily reached items.

- Save screenshots of the input and output as evidence that a random sample was drawn. Record how the population was subdivided and numbered for future reference.

Chapter 10

SAMPLE SIZE

Balancing the Need for Evidence with the Need for Information

There are invariably two pressures on auditors as they prepare themselves for fieldwork. The first pressure is the need for sufficient evidence to formulate an audit opinion. As risk increases, the need for more evidence also increases. As the quality of evidence increases, the need for additional corroborating evidence decreases. Examination of transactions is considered high-quality evidence. However, is it considered sufficient if the sample size in a given subset is very small? Spreading sample size over a large number of subsets compromises the high quality of the evidence of examining transactions. It is critical that if examining transactions (whether it be a random sample, selecting all transactions, or selecting specific transactions) is to be considered a high-quality type of evidence, there be sufficient transactions, particularly in the random sample, to support that contention.

The second pressure is to provide enough information to the client so that he or she can create action plans to correct any deficiencies the audit has found. At the outset, a sample size of 10 in a given subset appears to be relatively large. However, with a noncompliance rate of 10%, a single transaction will be handed over to the client to supply the necessary information for corrective action. Sample size should be balanced against the client's need for information.

Selecting a Sample Size—Cost versus Quantity and Quality of Evidence

If a statistical test is *not* being contemplated, sample size is driven by two factors—the cost to perform the examination of the transactions and the quantity and quality of evidence needed by the auditor. In its simplest form, sample size is just another resourcing requirement.

Sample size should fluctuate from audit to audit in response to risk levels and the quantity and quality of evidence from other sources. When there is sufficient evidence from other sources, sample size can be reduced. With less evidence available, sample size should be increased. Because examining transactions is both costly in terms of resources needed to examine the transactions and highly objective, this type of evidence should be reserved for high-risk subsets where a high level of assurance is required.

There is no perfect number for sample size, there is only the best sample size for the unique conditions of a specific audit. That being said, there are at present two sources of professional advice on sample size available for auditors.

The first is the PricewaterhouseCoopers (PwC) monograph of 2004. This article was written as guidance for management two years after the implementation of the U.S. Sarbanes-Oxley Act of 2002. **Table 10-1** and attached text was taken from this article.

Table 10-1: PricewaterhouseCoopers 2004 Recommended Sample Sizes		
Frequency of Manual Control's Performance	**Typical Number/ Range of Times to Test Controls**	**Factors to Consider when Deciding the Extent of Testing**
Multiple times a day	25 to 60	■ Complexity of the control
Daily	20 to 40	■ Significance of judgment in the control operation
Weekly	5 to 15	■ Level of competence necessary to perform the control
Monthly	2 to 5	■ Frequency of operation of the control
Quarterly	2	■ Impact of changes in volume or personnel performing the control
Annually	1	■ Importance of the control ☐ Addresses multiple assertions ☐ Period-end detective control ☐ Only control that covers a particular assertion

"The following table represents our view of the extent of testing necessary to support a conclusion that a manual control is operating effectively, provided no exceptions are found. The sample size that management decides to select for testing should be based on the significance of the control in question and level of assurance desired. The fewer items tested, the greater the risk of an incorrect conclusion. Thus, for highly critical controls, or when a single manual control provides the sole support for a financial statement assertion regarding a single account, we believe management should consider increasing its sample size to the high end of the range provided in the table above." (PricewaterhouseCoopers, 2004, pp. 61, 62).

The PwC sample size table is not a statistically derived table. In other words, the sample sizes were not created using a probability-based statistical formula, such as one used to perform a statistical test. Secondly, note that this is PwC's professional opinion about an appropriate sample size. Lastly, note that the sample sizes are expressed in ranges, not as single values. PwC clearly states that for critical controls or when the risk is high, a larger sample size should be considered. In other words, sample size is fluid. It should fluctuate as opposed to remaining as a static value, similar to the fluctuations in risk levels.

In 2009, the American Institute of Certified Public Accountants (AICPA) published "Audit Sampling Considerations of Circular A-133 Compliance Audits," which is the second source of professional guidance on sample size. Sample sizes are proposed separately for tests of controls and tests of compliance because the objectives of tests for controls and tests for compliance are different. However, as can be seen in **table 10-2** and **table 10-3**, the proposed sample sizes are identical.

Table 10-2: AICPA 2009, Sample Sizes for Tests of Controls	
Control Testing Sample Size Table	
Significance of Control and Inherent Risk of Compliance Requirement	**Minimum Sample Size**
	0 deviations expected
Very significant and higher inherent risk	60
Very significant and limited inherent risk or moderately significant and higher inherent risk	40
Moderately significant and limited inherent risk	25

Source: AICPA 2009, Audit Sampling Considerations of Circular A-133 Compliance Audits, p. 5.

Table 10-3: AICPA 2009, Sample Sizes for Tests of Compliance	
Compliance Testing Sample Size Table	
Desired Level of Assurance (Remaining Risk of Material Noncompliance)	**Minimum Sample Size**
	0 exceptions expected
High	60
Moderate	40
Low	25

Source: AICPA 2009, Audit Sampling Considerations of Circular A-133 Compliance Audits, p. 7.

AICPA emphasizes that these are minimum sample sizes and the auditor is expected to use professional judgment to increase the sample size, if warranted. Note the similarity between the PwC sample sizes proposed in 2004 and those proposed by AICPA in 2009.

In summary, auditors should use the guidance to provide a starting point for selecting their sample size. The following considerations need to be taken into account and the sample size adjusted accordingly:

1. The risk level of the subset(s) being examined. For very high-risk levels, sample size should be increased.

2. The quantity and quality of other evidence already collected and anticipated to be collected. If there is insufficient evidence, sample size should be increased. If there already is sufficient evidence (or there will be), sample size can be decreased.

3. The need of the client. If there is insufficient information for the client to be able to create corrective action, the sample size should be increased.

It should be noted that the sample sizes cited in **table 10-1**, **table 10-2**, and **table 10-3** are relatively small when compared to the sample sizes employed in applied research. This is because applied research relies solely on the statistical test as a single source of evidence to support or refute the statistical hypothesis. Auditors, on the other hand, rely on multiple sources of evidence to corroborate their findings. Consequently, smaller sample sizes are used and are balanced against the quantity and quality of other evidence collected.

Calculating a Sample Size

A sample size is calculated only when a statistical test is being contemplated. The usage of statistical tests in internal auditing has declined, even though there was a surge in popularity immediately after the implementation of Sarbanes-Oxley. The decline was most likely due to the large sample sizes required by most statistical tests. Sarbanes-Oxley-related audits (financial statement audits) are also experiencing a decline in the use of statistical tests.

Note that the professional guidance (PricewaterhouseCoopers, 2004; AICPA, 2009) does not require statistical tests to be performed, though most professional sources acknowledge that statistical tests could be performed if desired.

Attribute Sampling versus Variable Sampling

Attribute sampling refers to the situation in which the unit that composes the metric that is the focus of the statistical test (i.e., an error rate or noncompliance rate) can have only two different states. For example, a transaction is deemed to be either correct or incorrect, in compliance or not in compliance. Only two states exist for the transaction, even though the metric (the error rate or noncompliance rate) is expressed as a percentage that has multiple values.

Variable sampling refers to the situation in which the unit that composes the metric has multiple values, such as dollar value. External auditors frequently make use of variable sampling by taking a random sample, calculating a confidence interval, and comparing it to the recorded book value. If the recorded book value lies within the confidence interval, the auditor accepts the value within a specified level of confidence. If the book value lies outside the confidence interval, than an audit adjustment may be necessary.

With respect to statistical tests, attribute sampling is more commonly used by internal auditors and will be considered in detail in the following sections.

Three different distributions are currently used to calculate sample size. IDEA use the hypergeometric distribution, ACL uses the Poisson distribution, and many auditors use the binomial distribution.

The hypergeometric distribution is based on sampling without replacement. However, this requires relatively complex formulas that make it unsuitable unless it is supported by sufficient technology such as IDEA. The formula capabilities of Excel have alleviated this problem somewhat.

The Poisson distribution is based on sampling with replacement and relies on a relatively simple method of calculation for sample size. It is commonly used in dollar unit or monetary unit sampling.

The binomial distribution is also based on sampling with replacement. It uses a relatively simple calculation for sample size and is suitable for internal auditors who do not have access to technology such as IDEA or ACL or who wish to modify sample size while in the field.

In sample size calculations, Poisson-based sample sizes are larger than the binomial-based sample sizes, which are in turn larger than the hypergeometric-based sample sizes. With respect to confidence intervals, the Poisson-based intervals are larger than the binomial-based intervals, which are in turn larger than the hypergeometric-based intervals.

Binomial Estimation

The binomial distribution is the discrete probability distribution of the number of successes in a sequence of n independent yes/no experiments, each of which yields success with a probability p. The binomial distribution is the basis for the popular binomial test of statistical significance.

It is frequently used to model number of successes in a sample size n from a population of size N. Since the samples are not independent (as they would be with sampling without replacement), the resulting distribution is a hypergeometric distribution, not a binomial one. However, for N much larger than n, the binomial distribution is a good approximation and widely used. For large sample sizes, the binomial distribution very closely approximates the normal distribution.

To calculate the required sample size, the auditor must first chose appropriate values for the following statistical parameters.

Confidence Level – The most commonly used confidence level is 95%, which means that if 100 different random samples were drawn and confidence intervals were calculated for each random sample, 95 of the confidence intervals would contain the population parameter. Five of the confidence intervals would not contain the population parameter. Since it is not feasible or cost effective to draw 100 random samples, only one random sample is drawn. Unfortunately, the auditor will not know whether the single random sample that was drawn contains the population parameter or not. Reducing the confidence level to 90% means that the five confidence intervals that do not contain the population parameter now become 10 confidence intervals. In other words, the probability of obtaining a confidence interval that does *not* contain the population parameter has doubled.

Expected Error Rate – The expected error rate is the error rate that the auditor is expecting to find in the random sample. Currently, the industry best practice is between 3% and 5%. However, there are other sources of information about prospective expected error rates such as past audits, business entity policies, and directives and information from the client.

Margin of Error (Precision) – Margin of error is the interval around the expected error rate that is used to determine whether the hypothesis about the expected error rate (i.e., the value that was chosen for the expected error rate) is supported (if the error rate in the random sample is within the interval) or refuted (if the error rate in the random sample is outside the interval).

The formula used to calculate the sample size is as follows:

$$n = \frac{1.96^2 (p)(1-p)}{e^2}$$

Where 1.96 represents the constant for a 95% confidence interval, should you wish a 90% confidence level, the 1.96 is replaced with 1.645.

n = sample size

p = expected error rate

e = margin of error (precision)

Consider the calculated sample sizes for the following conditions:

CI = 95%, p = .02, e = .01, n = 753

CI = 95%, p = .05, e = .01, n = 1825

CI = 95%, p = .08, e = .01, n = 2827

CI = 95%, p = .05, e = .03, n = 203

CI = 95%, p = .05, e = .05, n = 73

As can be seen, the sample sizes are not small. As the expected error rate approaches 50%, sample size increases. A three-point increase from .02 to .05 in expected error rate resulted in an increase in sample size from 753 to 1,825. However, a slightly smaller increase in the margin of error for .01 to .03 resulted in a reduction of sample size from 1,825 to 203. The most effective way to manage sample size is to play off sample size against margin of error.

Another point of interest is the upper bound. This point is the upper limit of the confidence interval and is equal to the expected error rate plus the margin of error. The upper bound (or maximum tolerable error rate) is important because it represents the largest value of an error rate found in the random sample that would still support the hypothesized expected error rate. For example, for an expected error rate of 5% and a margin of error of 5%, the upper bound is 10%. The relationship between the expected error rate and the margin of error is often expressed as 5% +/-5%.

The upper bound is often the deciding factor as to whether to perform a statistical test. Consider the previous example. The intent of the statistical test would be to prove within a 95% confidence level that the population error rate is somewhere in the interval of 0% to 10%, which is another way of stating 5% +/-5%. Obviously management would want an error rate somewhere in the range of 3% to 5%. If the calculated error rate from the random sample is 10% (the upper bound), then the auditor is 95% confident that the error rate is somewhere in the interval of 0% to 10%. Management's difficulty (and the auditor's challenge) is to rationalize how a calculated 10% error rate, which in most instances would be considered unacceptable, is somehow supporting the contention that the population error rate may be in the more acceptable ranges of 3% to 5%.

The sample size to perform a statistical test of 5% +/-5% at the 95% confidence level is 73. Reducing the margin of error to +/-3% (an upper bound of 8%) results in a sample size of 203. Further reduction of the margin of error to +/-2% (an upper bound of 7%) increases the sample size to 456. Bringing the margin of error down to a suitably tight interval with an acceptable upper bound results in very large sample sizes.

The use of a random sample implies that the sample is probability based. In other words, there is always uncertainty about whether the single random sample selected by the researcher is truly representative of the population. To counter this uncertainty, the statistical conclusion quantifies the uncertainty in two ways. The first is the use of confidence level (in this case 95%), which quantifies the uncertainty around the selection of the random sample. The second is the margin of error (+/-Y%), which quantifies the uncertainty around the expected population proportion (expected error rate).

From an audit perspective, consider a situation with a 95% confidence level, an expected error rate of 4%, and a margin of error of 4%. The calculated sample size is 92. In scenario #1, the error rate calculated in the random sample of 92 transactions was 7%. In this instance, the statistical conclusion would be as follows:

"The auditor is 95% confident that the error rate in the population is 4% +/-4%."

In scenario #2, the error rate calculated in the random sample of 92 transactions was 10% and the corresponding statistical conclusion would be:

"The auditor is 95% confident that the error rate in the population is *not* 4% +/-4%."

Note that the distinction between scenario #1 and scenario #2 lies in the relative position of calculated error rate. In scenario #1, the calculated error rate from the random sample is within the interval created by adding and subtracting the margin of error from the expected error rate of 4%. In scenario #2, the calculated error rate from the random sample is outside the margin of error interval.

Consider for a moment that the population size for these two scenarios was 5,000 transactions. In scenario #2, the calculated error rate is outside the margin error interval and much larger than the industry best practice of 3% to 5%. The statistical conclusion tells the auditor that at a 95% confidence level, the error rate in the population is not 4% +/- 4%. Is the auditor's interest on the expected error rate of 4% or the calculated error rate of 10%? The distance between 4% and 10% is fairly large. It is doubtful that management needs a statistical test to tell them that 10% is not the same as 4%.

However, extrapolating the 10% onto the population (.1 x 5,000) yields 500 transactions that potentially have errors. Unfortunately, the statistical parameters, particularly the 95% confidence level and the margin of error, cannot be applied to the calculated error rate or the extrapolation. The statistical parameters are irrevocably tied to the expected error rate. In other words, the auditor cannot state that he or she is 95% confident that the population error rate is 10% or that there are 500 transactions that potentially have errors. The extrapolation is made possible because the 92 transactions were drawn randomly, not because a statistical test was performed.

The usefulness of statistical tests rests on their ability to discriminate between a hypothesized value and a calculated value that are very close to each other. However, the business relevance of the calculated error rate is in most cases more important than whether the calculated error rate is inside or outside a proscribed confidence interval.

The sole benefit of a statistical test is the statistical conclusion. This is why statistical tests are performed. Calculating a sample size based on preselected statistical parameters and then not stating the statistical conclusion means one of two things: a) the auditor has consciously chosen not to report the statistical test, or b) the auditor does not realize that the sole benefit of the statistical test is the statistical conclusion. There is no inherent benefit in a calculated sample size regardless of the original intent of the auditor if a statistical conclusion is not cited.

Adjustment for Population Size

A review of the binomial estimation formula indicates that there is no variable for population size.

$$n = \frac{1.96^2(p)(1-p)}{e^2}$$

One of the assumptions of the binomial estimation is that the population size is much larger than the sample size. It is for this reason that there is not a population variable in the formula. Adjustment of sample size based on population size is a cost reduction strategy. It is done in a situation in which the sample size is a significant portion of the population size. Adjustments to the sample size based on population size are only done when a statistical test is being performed. There would be no compelling reason to do this adjustment on a sample size that was not calculated using a statistical formula.

There are two formulas used to adjust the sample size based on population size (Cochran, 1977). Either one could be used and are multiplied against the calculated sample size once it has been calculated.

$$N/(N + n) \quad \text{or} \quad (N - n)/N$$

Note that the sample size will need to be 10% or greater of the population size before there is significant cost savings (i.e., reduction in the calculated sample size). Also note that if the calculated sample size is adjusted, the margin of error must be recalculated so that the mathematical relationship among the statistical parameters is maintained (see below).

The Relationship Among the Statistical Parameters

Sample size is calculated based on the binomial estimation formula.

$$n = \frac{1.96^2(p)(1-p)}{e^2}$$

The relationship among the confidence level, the expected error rate, the margin of error, and the sample size is defined by this formula and must be maintained. The confidence level and expected error rate are selected prior to commencing the random selection. Once data from the random sample has been selected and examined, it is inappropriate (bordering on unethical) to change either the confidence level or the expected error rate.

However, sample size frequently changes when transactions are examined for a variety of reasons ranging from a lack of resources to increasing sample size because of unforeseen circumstances. Regardless of the reason, at the end of data collection, before stating the statistical conclusion, the relationship among the statistical parameters must be reinstated, which means the margin of error must be recalculated. To do this, first solve the equation for e.

$$n = \frac{1.96^2(p)(1-p)}{e^2}$$

$$e^2 = \frac{1.96^2(p)(1-p)}{n}$$

$$e = \sqrt{\frac{1.96^2(p)(1-p)}{n}}$$

Use the final formula to calculate a new margin of error that is dictated by the actual sample size employed at the end of the audit.

Sample Size Allocation Strategies

Sample Frames

A sample frame is a simple method used to depict the different subsets that have been selected from a population of data. It typically holds subset population information such as the size of the subset and the total dollar value of all transactions in that subset. The primary use of sample frames is the allocation of sample size.

Currently in most audits, simple or stratified sample frames are used. In a simple sample frame (that corresponds to a single group), the decisions about sample size are very straightforward because splitting the sample size up among multiple groups is not an issue. The decision is reduced to how much resourcing to apply to the examination of transactions versus collecting other evidence.

The stratified sample frame is of greater concern in part due to its popularity and also to the various strategies employed in the allocation of sample size. Before considering those strategies, it warrants mentioning that allocation of sample size is very different from estimating sample size. The estimation of sample size is driven by cost and need for evidence or calculated using a statistical formula (if a statistical test is being performed). Allocation of sample size is driven by the strategy of how to allocate resourcing (sample size) and evidence need across the sample frame.

Three different sample allocation strategies are considered for the stratified sample frame. Each strategy has its advantages and disadvantages. Auditors should consider carefully the information that is available and the objectives of each sample allocation strategy.

Equal Weighted Design

The equal weighted design occurs when equal sample sizes are allocated to two or more subsets. The equal sample size implies that on some dimension, the two subsets are equal. It may be on such things as importance, such as a reporting requirement—clients, management, or the audit committee may require separate reports on each subset. Or it may be driven by equal risk levels such as the dollars at risk.

It is important that when equal sample sizes are allocated to two or more subsets, the auditors ask themselves, "What is equal?" If they are able to articulate what is equal, then they should go one step further and ask whether the two subsets should be kept separate or combined into a single subset. If it is not possible to determine what is equal, the auditors have not obtained sufficient information and should continue to gather information about the various subsets.

The major risk of this design is that it is so easy to implement. Because of the ease of implementation, there is a tendency to finalize the sample size allocation early in the audit when there is a minimum amount of information available to support the sample size allocation. In this instance, the equality represents what the auditor doesn't know. Equal weighted designs implemented in this manner are inefficient with the same sample size being allocated to both high-risk and low-risk subsets.

Proportional Weighted Design

Proportional allocation of sample size results in sample sizes allocated to cells proportional to the subset's population size. The simplest way to implement a proportional allocation of sample size is to draw the total sample size from all subsets (all subsets combined into a single population). Once the total sample size has been drawn, separate it into its component subsets. In this manner, proportionality is automatically instilled in the sample size for each individual subset.

This design has three distinct advantages. First, it allows the auditor to express an error rate or noncompliance rate for the total population without having to calculate a weighted average. Unfortunately, this advantage often outweighs whether the allocation design is the most appropriate design for the audit's objective. Second, the calculation of the overall error rate or noncompliance rate is simply the number of errors (or instances of noncompliance) divided by the total sample size. Third, individual subsets with large sample sizes can also be reported as separate findings. However, note that the sample size must be large enough to place reliance in the result. Sample sizes under 10 are subject to a great deal of variability, with a single error accounting for 10% or greater in the calculation of the subset's error rate.

Unfortunately this design has two distinct disadvantages that are often overlooked. First, all of the subsets that do not have sufficient sample size to report on separately only serve to provide coverage of the remaining parts of the population. The proportion of sample size used in this way may range as high as 15% to 20% of the total sample size and is called the cost of coverage. The question becomes whether having a total population estimate is worth the cost of coverage. A population estimate has the advantage of ease of communication and tracking year by year. However, it does not aid in identifying specific problems with controls or compliance. Clients should always know the cost of an overall population estimate. They may decide to support investing it in specific subsets they deem to be high risk rather than using the sample size for coverage.

Second, the basic assumption underlying the proportional allocation design is that risk is proportional to subset population size. This assumption manifests itself when subsets with a larger subset population have a larger sample size allocated to them. However, in financial data, the subsets with the largest subset population size contain the transactions with the lowest dollar values. If a proportional allocation design is applied directly to financial data, the subsets containing the lowest dollar transactions receive the majority of the sample size. However, if risk is assumed to be proportional to dollar value, the higher dollar value transactions are deemed to be higher risk and yet they receive proportionally less sample size allocated to them.

It is very important to understand exactly the nature of risk and how it relates to the various subsets under consideration, particularly when considering either the equal weighted design or the proportional weighted design. In some instances, it may be related to subset population size. In others, it is related to something else entirely such as a specific organizational unit or time period. One should never assume that because an overall population estimate of the error rate or noncompliance rate is being considered that a proportional weighted design is the only solution.

Risk-Based Design

In a risk-based design, the sample size is allocated proportional to the risk level of the subset. This depends on the auditor knowing the risk level of each subset and being able to prioritize the subsets based on risk level. This is necessarily done when the auditor has the maximum amount of information about the various subsets that have been identified.

Typically, the sample size allocation happens in the audit program at the same time as resources are allocated to the remaining methods of evidence collection that will occur during the fieldwork portion of the audit.

Case Study

Random.org

Random.org is an online random number generator that draws a random sample with replacement. This means that once a specific random selection has been performed, the item number is returned to the population and is available for subsequent selections. When the population size is very large, the probability of selecting the same item number a second time is very low. In this case, the integer generator application would be used. Simply enter the appropriate fields and the application will provide a random selection of item numbers. If the population is small (for example, less than 500 transactions), Random.org's sequence generator should be used. This application takes the total population of item numbers and places them in a random sequence. The sequence can be copied and pasted into an Excel spreadsheet beside the data of concern. Sorting the data set based on the sequence generated numbers will rearrange the population into a random sequence.

To Begin	■ Use your browser to search for Random.org.
	■ Scroll down to FREE Services – Numbers.
	■ If your population is relatively large (i.e., greater than 500, the probability of having duplicates in the random sample is minimal), go to integer generator.
	■ If your population is relatively small (i.e., less than 500, the probability of having duplicates in the random sample is increased), go to sequence generator.
Integer Generator	■ Follow the instructions – Part 1: The Integers.
	■ Generate x random integers refers to the sample size.
	■ Each integer should have a value between x and y refers to the population size. If your population is in an Excel spreadsheet, the first number in the integer generator is the first row number with your data. The second number is the last row number in the spreadsheet containing your data.
	■ Choose an appropriate format for displaying the results.
	■ The output represents the row numbers of the items that are to be randomly selected.
Sequence Generator	■ Follow the instructions – Part 1: Sequence Boundaries.
	■ Smallest value – typically 1 regardless of the row number of your first item in your data set.
	■ Largest value – typically the total size of the population.
	■ Format – use one column if possible – the output is a single of list of "x" numbers (where x is the population size) in a random sequence.
	■ Cut and paste the column of random numbers into a column directly adjacent to your data set.
	■ Sort the complete data set based on the column of random numbers.
	■ Start at the top of the sorted data set and count down until your sample size is reached.

Allocation of Sample Size in an Equal Weighted Design

The allocation of sample size must take into account the subsets created as a result of the analytical procedures. In an equal weighted design, the sample size would be equally spread over all subsets that were deemed to be too large to allow examination of all items in the subset. In other words, subsets corresponding to select all items and select specific items (typically there are not a large number of potentially fraudulent items) would not be included. Consequently, a random sample would not be drawn in each of these subsets.

Of the five subsets identified in the Oklahoma data, three have sub-population sizes that in most cases would prohibit examining all items in the subset. Two subsets (greater than $60,000) are sufficiently small enough to allow examination in their entirety.

Consider a total sample size of 50. Fourteen items would be allocated to the two subsets greater than $60,000, leaving 36 items for the random selection.

In an equal weighted design, the 36 items would be spread equally across the three subsets from which random samples would be drawn, resulting in each subset having a sample size of 12 (see **table 10-4**).

Table 10-4: Equal Weighted Design - Allocation of Sample Size to High-Risk Subsets		
2012–2013 P-Card Expenditures	**University of Oklahoma**	**University of Oklahoma Health Sciences Center**
Greater than $10,000 and less than $60,000	N = 188 Total Dollar Value = $3,880,965.20 n = 12	N = 117 Total Dollar Value = $2,546,358.34 n = 12
Greater than $60,000	N = 7 Total Dollar Value = $4,583,856.62	N = 7 Total Dollar Value = $2,381,198.75
Last two weeks of June 2012	N = 575 Total Dollar Value = $116,273.32 n = 12	

Remember that a risk assessment would have been completed on these cells and therefore there would have been an additional layer of information in addition to total dollar value. The challenge with the equal weighted design is that it treats all subsets as being equal. For example, it equates the University of Oklahoma greater than $10,000 and less than $60,000 subset, which has a total dollar value of $3,880,965.20 with University of Oklahoma's last two weeks of June, which has total dollar value of $116,273.32. At the end of the sample size allocation, the auditors should always ask themselves if the sample size is being allocated so that they are getting value for money.

Allocation of Sample Size in a Proportional Weighted Design

Using the same Oklahoma data as above, the sample sizes have now been adjusted to show a proportional distribution. The total number of transactions within each of the three larger subsets was expressed as a ratio of the total number of transactions in all three subsets. The ratio multiplied by the remaining sample size of 36 yielded the individual subset sample sizes (see **table 10-5**).

Table 10-5: Proportional Weighted Design - Allocation of Sample Size to High-Risk Subsets		
2012–2013 P-Card Expenditures	**University of Oklahoma**	**University of Oklahoma Health Sciences Center**
Greater than $10,000 and less than $60,000	N = 188 Total Dollar Value = $3,880,965.20 n = 8	N = 117 Total Dollar Value = $2,546,358.34 n = 5
Greater than $60,000	N = 7 Total Dollar Value = $4,583,856.62	N = 7 Total Dollar Value = $2,381,198.75
Last two weeks of June 2012	N = 575 Total Dollar Value = $116,273.32 n = 23	

A fully proportional design means that the subsets with the smallest number of transactions will have proportionally less sample size allocated to them. Note that the two subsets greater than $10,000 and less than $60,000 represent the tails of the frequency distributions for the University Oklahoma and the University of Oklahoma Health Sciences Center. The auditor should decide whether allocating only 13 sample items to these two subsets adequately deals with the risk represented by these two subsets.

The challenge in the proportional design is that the largest subsets in terms of population size use the majority of the sample size. Since sample size is directly proportional to the amount of resourcing needed to examine the items, sample size is always finite. **Table 10-6** lists the results of a proportional allocation of 36 to subsets based only on the frequency cut points. Note that no sample size would be allocated to the smaller subsets.

Table 10-6: University of Oklahoma and University of Oklahoma Health Sciences Center 2012–2013 Subsets Frequencies		
Frequency Interval	**University of Oklahoma**	**University of Oklahoma Health Sciences Center**
Less than $10,000	N = 78823 n = 21	N = 55806 n = 15
Greater than $10,000 and less than $60,000	N = 188 n = 0	N = 117 n = 0
Greater than $60,000	N = 7 n = 0	N = 7 n = 0

The skewed allocation of sample size is a direct function of the shape of the skewed distribution. In the case of the university, data listed above 99.7% of the transactions are less than $10,000. This is consistent with the total population of the State of Oklahoma data that has 99.5% of their expenditures less than $5,000. The skewed shape of the distribution is not unusual.

The major challenge with this design is to consider the subsets with little or no sample size and consider their risk levels. Do these subsets warrant increased sample size due to their higher risk levels? Or should they be left with a minimal sample size? Or should they be removed? It is these questions that make the allocation of sample size a difficult decision.

Allocation of Sample Size in a Risk-Based Design

Had a risk assessment been performed as part of this case study, the auditor would be able to prioritize the subsets based on a much more complete view of the risk levels. That being said, for the purposes of this example, assume that risk level is proportional to the total dollar value for each subset. The two subsets greater than $60,000, were examined in their entirety, in part due to the size of their total dollar values and in part due to the small number of transactions contained in each subset. For the remaining subsets, sample size was allocated based on the ratio of the total dollar value of the subset divided by the total dollar value of all subsets (excluding the two subsets greater than $60,000). See **table 10-7**.

Table 10-7: Risk-Based Design #1 - Allocation of Sample Size to High-Risk Subsets		
2012–2013 P-Card Expenditures	University of Oklahoma	University of Oklahoma Health Sciences Center
Greater than $10,000 and less than $60,000	N = 188 Total Dollar Value = $3,880,965.20 n = 21	N = 117 Total Dollar Value = $2,546,358.34 n = 14
Greater than $60,000	N = 7 Total Dollar Value = $4,583,856.62	N = 7 Total Dollar Value = $2,381,198.75
Last two weeks of June 2012	N = 575 Total Dollar Value = $116,273.32 n = 1	

It can be seen in the Risk-Based Design #1 that the subset for the last two weeks of June 2012 received a sample size of 1. It is at this point that another major learning takes place. Using mathematics such as proportions (whether it be based on number of transactions or total dollar value) only goes so far. *At some point, the auditor is forced into a position where he or she must make some professional judgments.* This is one such instance. Is the subset for the last two weeks of June 2012 of greater or lesser importance? The total dollar value is low compared to the other subsets. However, the subset represents an unusual number of transactions occurring during the last week of June.

Assume that the transactions in the last two weeks of June 2012 are important. The sample size to examine must come from somewhere. **Table 10-8** shows a second sample frame that presents another alternative.

Table 10-8: Risk-Based Design #2 - Allocation of Sample Size to High-Risk Subsets		
2012–2013 P-Card Expenditures	University of Oklahoma	University of Oklahoma Health Sciences Center
Greater than $10,000 and less than $60,000	N = 305 Total Dollar Value = $6,427,232.54 n = 20	
Greater than $60,000	N = 7 Total Dollar Value = $4,583,856.62	N = 7 Total Dollar Value = $2,381,198.75
Last two weeks of June 2012	N = 575 Total Dollar Value = $116,273.32 n = 16	

In this design, the two subsets for greater than $10,000 and less than $60,000 for the University of Oklahoma and the University of Oklahoma Health Sciences Center were combined. Combination is one of two strategies used to help reduce the sample frame down to something that is more manageable. Combining two subsets allows for the same coverage as before and the use of a smaller overall sample size. The freed-up sample size was allocated to the last two weeks of June 2012.

Why is reduction of the number of subsets so important? First, as was mentioned previously, every audit has a limited number of resources than can be expended on examining transactions. Second, it counter-balances the auditor's inherent desire to look at everything. The intent of reduction is not to remove subsets so that they are not examined. Rather it is to identify the critical few subsets that can be subjected to an examination of transactions, which is the most costly evidence collection method. The subsets that are removed from the sample frame are evaluated under a different type of evidence, which may involve everything from interviews to process walkthroughs.

Increasing the Sample Size

The auditor may come across some unexpected findings during the selection and examination of items. This could be a higher error rate than expected, or a specific control that has been compromised, or something softer such as a lack of training or clarity on procedures. Whatever the reason, the auditor is faced with the decision of whether or not to examine more items.

Note that this only applies to random selection. The remaining subsets (selecting all items and selecting specific items) were examined in their entirety and as such there are no remaining items left to be examined. Within random selection, extending the sample size (as in randomly selecting additional items) is not a problem provided that a) the boundaries of the population have not been changed, and b) if a statistical test is being performed, the confidence level and expected error rate have not been changed.

The simplest way to increase a random selection, particularly in the field, is to use Random.org to select the additional items. If the sequence generator was used in the original selection, continue down the list from the point where the original sample size terminated until sufficient additional sample size has been selected. For larger populations (i.e., greater than 500 items), use the integer generator to select additional items. If an item has already been examined, simply skip it and move on to the next one.

Increasing the sample size as a solution to unexpected findings is typically driven by one of two desires. The first is to validate the error rate, which in this instance would be unexpectedly high. The most efficient and effective method of increasing the sample size to meet this desire is to extend the random selection, as described above.

The second desire is to provide more information to the client so that they are better able to formulate corrective action plans. In this case, random selection may not be the most efficient solution. Consider a 10% error rate. It would take a random selection of 10 items to identify a single error for the client to use. It would be more appropriate (if sufficient information is available) to select specific transactions that meet the criteria identified from the failed transactions/items already selected. This action would result in the creation of a separate subset (select specific items) that is not based on random selection.

Note that in most cases, the selection of specific transactions or items that meet specific criteria (such as fraud red flags) is performed in advance of the random selection. This will keep the specific transactions/items separate from the randomly selected transactions/items so that there is no double counting. However, while identifying and selecting the random transactions/ items, the auditors should always keep their eyes open for unusual or suspicious transactions or items (i.e., those meeting specific criteria such as fraud red flags). If a transaction or item is discovered that meets these specific criteria, it is selected and placed in the subset for selecting specific items and *not* in the random sample. *The only exception to the above is if the transaction or item meeting those specific criteria has already been identified as part of the random sample, it must remain as part of the random sample.*

Summary – What's Important

Estimating Sample Size

- Sample size is driven by two factors—cost and the need for evidence.

- The most notable difference between an applied research model and an audit model is that an applied research model relies on a single source of evidence (the statistical test) and an audit model relies on multiple sources of evidence. Consequently, sample sizes used in audits are typically smaller than those used in applied research.

- Sample size is not static—it should fluctuate depending on the risk level of the subset and the need for sufficient evidence.

- There is professional guidance available on sample size (PricewaterhouseCoopers 2004, AICPA 2009).

Calculating Sample Size

- Sample size is only calculated when a statistical test is being contemplated.

- The statistical parameters (confidence level, margin of error) are tied to the *expected error rate* and cannot be reported in conjunction with the *calculated error rate* from the random sample.

- There must always be a mathematical relationship among the statistical parameters. If the sample size has changed from the originally calculated sample size for any reason, the margin of error must be recalculated.

Sample Size Allocation Strategies

- Whenever auditors find themselves in a position where equal sample sizes have been allocated to two or more cells, they should determine what the equality represents. If the subsets are truly equal, they should consider combining them.

- Care must be taken in the use of a proportional design to ensure that *risk is proportional to population frequency*. Financial data is typically skewed, which means that some subsets may have relatively small numbers of transactions in them. In a proportional allocation, these subsets would be underrepresented (i.e., little or no sample size would be allocated to them).

- Risk-based designs allow the allocation of sample size to be proportional to risk levels. Proportionality can be restored through the use of a weighted average (see chapter 11).

Increasing Sample Size

- Sample size can be increased provided:
  - ☐ The boundaries of the population have not been changed; and
  - ☐ If a statistical test is being performed, the confidence level and expected error rate have been changed.

Chapter 11

COMBINING THE RESULTS

More often than not, audits contain a combination of subsets that were examined in their entirety (select specific items and/or select all items) and subsets that were subjected to random sampling. This is particularly true because of the necessity for auditors to include examination for fraud in all of their audits.

The scenario becomes slightly more complicated if a risk-based sample frame is employed in the audit. In this case, the sample size is allocated proportional to the level of risk.

Sometimes management, the client, or audit committee would like to see a combined error rate or noncompliance rate across all of the subsets that were examined. The auditor is now faced with how to restore proportionality so that the result is once again proportional to population sizes—while at the same time combining the random-based subsets with the subsets that were examined in their entirety.

Terminology

A variety of terminology will be used in the case study. Note the following:

1. Subscripts refer to subset number.

2. Uppercase indicates a population variable.

3. Lowercase indicates a sample variable.

Note the nomenclature used below. In order to combine the information from each subset, the following information will be needed:

1. **Raw Errors ($\tilde{e}$ $\tilde{E}$)** – the number of incorrect transactions

2. **Error Rates (p, ER_{pop})** – the number of incorrect transactions expressed as a percentage (raw errors divided by sample size equals error rate)

3. **Dollars at Risk (r, R)** – for each incorrect item, the dollars at risk (those dollars that may be lost, misspent, put in the wrong accounts, etc. if the control failure was not identified) is specified

4. **Population Size (N_1, N_2, N)** – the size of the population by subset or in total

5. **Sample Size (n_1, n_2, n)** – the size of the sample by subset or in total

6. **Dollar Values ($\$_{n1}$, $\$_{n2}$, $\$_1$, $\$_2$, $\$$)** – the total dollar value of all items in the sample or in the population either as a total or by subset

Note that dollars at risk must be identified once an individual transaction has been identified as a control failure or noncompliant. There is not a one-to-one correspondence between dollars at risk and error rate. For example, consider a business entity that has a policy to travel economy when traveling on company business. An audit of expense claims reveals an employee who traveled first class to attend a business meeting in another city. The dollars at risk is the difference between a first class fare and an economy fare. The business trip still had to occur; therefore, provided the additional expenses are compliant, the remainder of the claim is valid. *Note that it is incorrect to multiply the calculated error rate against the total dollar value of the population to determine the dollars at risk.*

How to Combine the Results

Once all of the selected transactions have been examined, an error rate will be calculated for each subset. Consider an example that has four subsets that were subjected to random sampling and two subsets that were examined in their entirety. Combining the results from a group of distinct subsets requires several computational steps. It is important that the steps be performed in sequence. The four steps are described below and then applied to the results of an expense claim audit.

Step 1: Combine the subsets that were subjected to random selection to a) restore proportionality, and b) create a single error rate that is proportionally representative of the total group of subsets that experienced random selection. This step is important because proportionality must be restored, particularly if a risk-based design was employed. Secondly, the random samples must be combined before their results are extrapolated onto the full population.

To perform this step, a weighted average is used. In this example there are four random subsets.

$$\frac{N_1(p_1) + N_2(p_2) + N_3(p_3) + N_4(p_4)}{N_{1+2+3+4}} = ER_{1+2+3+4}$$

Where:

- N_1, N_2, N_3, N_4 are population sizes for each subset
- p_1, p_2, p_3, p_4 are calculated error rates for each subset
- $N_{1+2+3+4}$ is the total population size for all of the random subsets combined
- $ER_{1+2+3+4}$ is the combined calculated error rate for the four random subsets

Step 2: Once the combined calculated error rate for the four random subsets has been calculated ($ER_{1+2+3+4}$), it is extrapolated on to the combined total of the four population sizes from which the random cells were drawn ($N_{1+2+3+4}$) to yield the number of transactions that potentially have errors.

$$(ER_{1+2+3+4}) \, (N_{1+2+3+4}) = \tilde{E}_{1+2+3+4}$$

Step 3: Assume that there are two subsets that were examined in their entirety (select specific items, select all items, or a combination of both) and label them subset 5 and subset 6. The number of raw errors for each of these subsets is already known (it was determined when the transactions were examined). Add the raw errors for these two subsets to the raw errors calculated in Step 2. It is critical that this combination be performed using raw errors and not percentages.

$$\tilde{E}_{1+2+3+4} + \tilde{E}_5 + \tilde{E}_6 = \tilde{E}_{1+2+3+4+5+6}$$

Step 4: Calculate the ratio of the total number of raw errors ($\tilde{E}_{1+2+3+4+5+6}$) divided by the total population size, including subsets 5 and 6 ($N_{1+2+3+4} + N_5 + N_6$).

$$\frac{\tilde{E}_{1+2+3+4+5+6}}{N_{1+2+3+4} + N_5 + N_6} = ER_{1+2+3+4+5+6} = ER_{pop}$$

Note that the weighted average in Step 1 has coefficients in the numerator that correspond to the population size of each of the subsets and that the denominator is composed of the total population size of the subsets that form the numerator. This relationship where the sum of the coefficients is equal to the denominator is a characteristic of a weighted average.

In order to create a weighted average of calculated error rates, population sizes must be used as coefficients. In the case study, a weighted average for dollars at risk (which is calculated in exactly the same manner) is shown, which uses total dollar amounts as coefficients.

The weighted average restores proportionality among the subsets that were subjected to random sampling. Combining raw errors from the combined randomly sampled subsets (Step 2) with raw errors from the subsets examined in their entirety (Step 3) ensures that proportionality is maintained.

Case Study: Audit of Expense Claims

Consider a four-cell audit design to examine expense claims. It was decided to limit the scope of the audit to only executive and management. The population was defined as all expense claims during the year of 2010 for executive and management. The information that was collected is shown in **table 11-1**.

Table 11-1: Audit of Expense Claims		
	Executive	**Management**
Over $10000	$N_1 = 27$ $\$_1 = \$300,000$	$N_2 = 3$ $\$_2 = \$30,500$
Under $10000	$N_3 = 150$ $\$_3 = \$500,000$	$N_4 = 600$ $\$_4 = \$1,500,000$

$$N = 780$$

$$\$ = \$2,330,500$$

There are four subsets, each with different population sizes and total dollar values. There are two subsets (executive and management claims above $10,000) in which the total number of transactions is small; therefore, it was decided that all transactions will be examined. This is an example of select all items.

The audit of expense claims for a particular business entity began with the data listed in **table 11-1**. A sample frame was created and is shown in **table 11-2**. It is based on a sample size of 140, which is on the very large size, but it makes the calculations easier to follow than smaller sample sizes. The two subsets containing expense claims greater than $10,000 were combined to form a single subset. These cells could easily have been kept separate and likely would be from a reporting perspective. However, for combining results, these two subsets will need to be combined in Step 3. From a statistical perspective, whether the subset is select specific items or select all items, mathematically they are treated in exactly the same manner.

Table 11-2: Sample Frame for Audit of Expense Claims		
	Executive	**Management**
Over $10,000	Select All Items $N_{1+2} = 30$	
Under $10,000	Random Sample $n_3 = 40$	Random Sample $n_4 = 70$

For this audit, the following data was collected and is shown in **table 11-3**.

Table 11-3: Tabulation of Results		
	Executive	**Management**
Over $10,000	$N_{1+2} = 30$ $\$_{1+2} = \$330,500$ $P_{1+2} = 16.7\%$ $\tilde{E}_{1+2} = 5$ $R_{1+2} = \$90,000$	
Under $10,000	$N_3 = 150$ $\$_3 = \$500,000$ $n_3 = 40$ $\$_{n3} = \$150,000$ $p_3 = 17.5\%$ $\tilde{e}_3 = 7$ $r_3 = \$55,000$	$N_4 = 600$ $\$_4 = \$1,500,000$ $n_4 = 70$ $\$_{n4} = \$180,000$ $p_4 = 5.7\%$ $\tilde{e}_4 = 4$ $r_4 = \$10,000$

Calculating a Combined Error Rate

Step 1: Combining Calculated Error Rates

Since error rates are a form of frequency, the weighting factors are subset population sizes. Note that the error rate has already been expressed as a percentage relative to sample size. The following formula should be used:

$$\frac{N_3(p_3) + N_4(p_4)}{N_{3+4}}$$

$$= \frac{(150)(.175) + (600)(.057)}{750}$$

$$= .081 \text{ or } 8.1\% = P_{3+4}$$

Step 2: Extrapolate to Find the Number of Raw Errors

$$\tilde{E}_{3+4} = (P_{3+4})(N_{3+4}) = (.081)(750) = 61$$

Step 3: Sum the Raw Errors

$$\tilde{E}_{1+2} = 5$$

$$\tilde{E}_{1+2} + \tilde{E}_{3+4} = 61 + 5 = 66$$

Step 4: Calculate the Total Population Error Rate

$$\frac{\tilde{E}_{1+2} + \tilde{E}_{3+4}}{N_{1+2+3+4}} = \frac{66}{780} = .085 \text{ or } 8.5\%$$

Calculating a Combined Dollars at Risk

Step 1: Combining Dollars at Risk

The dollars at risk has not been displayed as a ratio relative to the total dollar value of the sample. This is necessary in order to calculate a combined dollars at risk. The weighting factors for this calculation are cell and population dollar values. The following formula should be used:

$$\frac{\$_3(r_3/\$n_3) + \$_4(r_4/\$n_4)}{\$_{3+4}}$$

$$= \frac{(500,000)(55,000/150,000) + (1,500,000)(10,000/180,000)}{2,000,000}$$

$$= .13 \text{ or } 13\%$$

Step 2: Extrapolate to Find the Dollars at Risk

To calculate the actual dollars at risk:

$$(.13)(2,000,000) = \$260,000 = R_{3+4}$$

Step 3: Sum the Dollars at Risk

Since the dollars at risk is already in units of dollars, simply add together:

$$R = R_{1+2} + R_{3+4} = \$90,000 + \$260,000 = \$350,000$$

Step 4: Calculate the Total Population Dollar at Risk proportion

This value can also be expressed as a percentage of the total population dollar value:

$$\$350,000 / \$2,330,500 = 15\%$$

Summary – What's Important

- If the desire is to report a combined error rate or noncompliance rate, proportionality must be restored before combining the subsets with random selection with those that were examined in their entirety.

- Use a weighted average to restore proportionality and combine the subsets that were subjected to random selection together.

- Extrapolate the combined error rate onto the population size from which the random samples were drawn.

- Add the raw errors (not the percentages) from the extrapolation with the raw errors from the cells that were examined in their entirety.

- Re-express the raw errors as a ratio of the total population size.

- Dollars at risk must be identified when the transaction in question is being examined. It cannot be calculated after the fact. More specifically, the calculated error rate cannot be multiplied by the total dollar amount to create the dollars at risk.

- Combining dollars at risk results is done exactly the same way as combining error rates.

LESSONS LEARNED

I finish this book with some important lessons that I (re)learned as I tackled the State of Oklahoma data.

Foster your creativity and curiosity. Don't let the size of the data set overwhelm you. It is, after all, just a bunch of rows with data fields. Instead, set your doubts aside and enjoy the moment as you explore the data and develop an approach that will simplify the job ahead of you.

Make a plan and stick to it. It is so easy to get lost in a data set as the various possibilities and potential findings lead you down a never-ending path. And then two weeks later you will surface and realize that you have discovered a dozen potential fraud items, but the remaining 20 million transactions are still awaiting your attention. Develop a plan that contains logical steps on how to perform the data analysis. You will find interesting transactions along the way—note them, set them aside, and then get back to the plan.

Risk is the key. Risk is the foundation of the whole audit. It is key to subdivision, but it also links the audit objectives to the data analysis, the sampling strategies, the allocation of resources, and the findings. Without risk, the audit is a ship without a rudder, totally at the mercy of wayward thoughts from both auditors and clients alike. Carry risk with you, and whenever you feel you may be losing your direction, go back to risk to get back on track.

Look at the findings of the data analysis from both the graphical/tabular and metric perspectives. Results from analytical procedures are seldom so clear that they are black versus white. More often they are 50 or more shades of grey. Examining the data from several different perspectives allows you to see different pieces of the puzzle, and the excitement happens when the pieces fit together. Each graph, scatter plot, and metric provides a slightly different perspective and an additional piece of information. Individually, they may amount to little—together, they show a more complete picture.

Validate, validate, validate. Once you have found something, always validate it. Validate your benchmarks so that you can be certain they portray low risk and no unusual conditions that might have altered the data. When a high-risk subset has been identified, validate its risk level with management. When a major finding is discovered through examination of transactions/items, validate with management. Having management informed and cooperative is just as important as the discovery of a major finding.

Organize the data analysis results. Nothing is more embarrassing or frustrating than knowing that you have found something but can't produce the specific graph or metric. Large data sets will have a lot of subdivisions and consequently a lot of data analysis. Organize the results, whether through separate spreadsheets or tabs, so that they can be easily found and referenced.

Always trust your knowledge, your experience, and your intuition. Data analysis and sampling are not a black and white science, rather they are simply tools that auditors use in the performance of their duties. Much like a paintbrush is used to create a painting, the success relies on the knowledge, experience, and intuition of the auditor. Learn to trust what you bring to the table and use it as a lens to view your findings. Never assume that statistical tools are infallible.

Business relevance. At the end of the day, if the audit has not moved the business entity forward, it has been a waste of ink. Statistical tools and techniques are totally insensitive to business relevance. Linking the results of the data analysis and sampling strategies to business relevance cannot be done through the use of a piece of software or a statistical test. Only the auditor can make that connection. Never underestimate the value you bring to the audit.

REFERENCES

Chapter 1
Introduction

1. Implementation Guides, International Professional Practices Framework, Standard 2320 – Analysis and Evaluation. 2017. Lake Mary, FL: The Institute of Internal Auditors.

2. Public Company Accounting Oversight Board, Auditing Standard No. 1105, Audit Evidence, effective date December 15, 2010.

3. Oklahoma State P-Card data: https://data.ok.gov/dataset/purchase-card-pcard-fiscal-year-2014/resource/e2ebee55-73ac-46d4-984e-ba4874ef2593#{viewgrid:{columnsWidth:[{column:!Year-Month,width:134},{column:!Agency++Number,width:139},{column:!Agency++Name,width:147},{column:!Cardholder++Last++Name,width:165},{column:!Description,width:145},{column:!Amount,width:116},{column:!Vendor,width:166}]}}

4. OECD. 2014. Regulatory Enforcement and Inspections, OECD Best Practice Principles for Regulatory Policy, OECD Publishing.

Chapter 5
Frequency Analysis Case Study

1. State of Oklahoma Office of Management and Enterprise Services Policies and Procedures, P-Card Program, effective date of policy April 05, 2016.

Chapter 6
Time Series Analysis

1. Keith, V. 1972. *Design and Analysis in Experimentation*. University of Ottawa Press.

Chapter 9
Selecting Items for Testing

1. Hall, T., J. Hunton, and B. Pierce. 2000. The Use of and Selection Biases Associated with Non-Statistical Sampling in Auditing. *Behavioral Research in Accounting* 12: 231–255.

2. Hall, T., T. Herron, B. Pierce, and T. Witt. 2001 The Effectiveness of Increasing Sample Size to Mitigate the Influence of Population Characteristics in Haphazard Sampling. *Auditing: A Journal of Practice & Theory* 20 (1): 169–185.

3. Hall, T., T. L. Herron, and B. Pierce. 2006. How Reliable Is Haphazard Sampling? *The CPA Journal* 76 (1).

4. Hall, T., A. Higson, B. Pierce, K. Price, and C. Skousen. 2012. Haphazard Sampling: Selection Biases Induced by Control Listing Properties and the Estimation Consequences of These Biases. *Behavioral Research in Accounting* 24 (2): 101–132.

5. Hall, T., A. Higson, B. Pierce, K. Price, and C. Skousen. 2013. Haphazard Sampling: Selection Biases and the Estimation Consequences of These Biases. *Current Issues in Auditing* 7 (2): 16–22.

Chapter 10
Sample Size

1. PricewaterhouseCoopers. July 2004. Sarbanes-Oxley: Section 404, Practical Guidance for Management.

2. American Institute of Certified Public Accountants. Audit Sampling Considerations of Circular A-133 Compliance Audits, 009.

3. Cochran, William G. 1977. *Sampling Techniques.* John Wiley & Sons.

INTERNAL AUDIT FOUNDATION
SPONSOR RECOGNITION

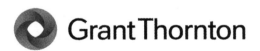

GOLD PARTNERS (US $5,000–$14,999)

Natarajan Girija Shankar,
CIA

Paul J. Sobel,
CIA, CRMA, QIAL

INTERNAL AUDIT FOUNDATION
LEADERSHIP SOCIETY MEMBERS

Eric Allegakoen, CIA, CCSA, CRMA

Doug Anderson, CIA, CRMA

Urton Anderson, CIA, CCSA, CFSA, CGAP, CRMA

Narendra Kumar Aneja, CIA, CRMA

Farah G. Araj, CIA, QIAL

Audley Bell, CIA

Lily Bi, CIA, QIAL, CRMA

Ben Bouchillon, CCSA

Karen Brady, CIA, CRMA

Judith K. Burke, CCSA

Mark Carawan, CIA, QIAL

Raven Catlin, CIA, CFSA, CRMA

Richard F. Chambers, CIA, QIAL, CCSA, CGAP, CRMA

Angelina Chin, CIA, CCSA, CRMA

Brian Christensen

Daniel Clayton, CIA

Ann Cohen

Andrew Dahle, CIA, CRMA

Gary Daugherty, CIA

Scott Feltner, CIA

Philip E. Flora, CIA, CCSA

Brian Foster, CIA

Michael J. Fucilli, CIA, QIAL, CGAP, CRMA

Steve Goepfert, CIA, QIAL, CRMA

Nancy Haig, CIA, CCSA, CFSA, CRMA

Lawrence J. Harrington, CIA, QIAL, CRMA

Lisa Hartkopf

Eric Hespenheide

Glenn Ho, CIA, CRMA

Pamela Jenkins, CIA, CRMA

Bailey Jordan, CIA, CRMA

Mike Joyce, CIA, CRMA

Tina Kim, CIA, CGAP, CRMA

Deborah Kretchmar, CIA

Michael J. Lynn, CRMA

Betty McPhilimy, CIA, CRMA

Raoul Menes, CIA, CCSA, CRMA

William (Bill) Michalisin

Patricia Miller, CIA, QIAL, CRMA

James A. Molzahn, CIA, CRMA

Naohiro Mouri, CIA

Karla Munden, CIA, QIAL, CCSA, CFSA, CRMA

Michael Newman, CIA

Frank M. O'Brien, CIA, QIAL

Carey Oven, CIA

J. Michael (Mike) Peppers, CIA, QIAL, CRMA

Cynthia G. Plamondon, CIA, QIAL, CCSA, CFSA, CGAP, CRMA

Charles Redding

Anthony Ridley, CIA

Michael P. Rose, CIA, CCSA, CRMA

Debra Roth, CIA

Stanley Rubins

Mark Salamasick, CIA, CGAP, CRMA

Thomas Sanglier II, CIA, CRMA

Kimberly Schroeder, CIA

N.G. Shankar, CIA

Alan N. Siegfried, CIA, CCSA, CFSA, CGAP, CRMA

Harold C. Silverman, CIA, QIAL, CRMA

Paul J. Sobel, CIA, QIAL, CRMA

Jared Soileau, CIA, CCSA, CRMA, and
Laura Soileau, CIA, CRMA

Tania Stegemann, CIA, CCSA, CRMA

Warren Stippich, CIA, CRMA

Carrie Summerlin, CCSA

Gerard Totton, CIA, QIAL

Bonnie L. Ulmer

Dominique Vincenti, CIA, CRMA

Jacqueline Wagner, CIA

Angela Witzany, CIA, QIAL, CRMA

Charles Wright, CIA

Benito Ybarra, CIA

Douglas Ziegenfuss, CIA, CCSA, CRMA

MEMBERS

Kevin L. Cantrell, CIA, *Plains All American Pipeline*

Stephen D. Goepfert, CIA, CRMA, QIAL

Ulrich Hahn, CIA, CCSA, CGAP, CRMA

Lisa Hartkopf, *Ernst & Young LLP*

Steven E. Jameson, CIA, CCSA, CFSA, CRMA, *Community Trust Bank*

Pamela Short Jenkins, CIA, CRMA, *Fossil, Inc.*

Tow Toon Lim, CRMA, *DSO National Laboratories*

James A. Molzahn, CIA, CRMA, *Sedgwick, Inc.*

Frank M. O'Brien, CIA, QIAL, *Olin Corporation*

Sakiko Sakai, CIA, CCSA, CFSA, CRMA, *Infinity Consulting*

Anton Van Wyk, CIA, CRMA, QIAL, *PricewaterhouseCoopers LLP*

Yi Hsin Wang, CIA, CGAP, CRMA, *National Taipei University*

Ana Cristina Zambrano Preciado, CIA, CCSA, CRMA, *IIA–Colombia*

Judy Gunther, CIA, CRMA

Yulia Gurman, CIA, *Packaging Corporation of America*

Beatrice Ki-Zerbo, CIA, *ifaci, Paris, France*

Mani Massoomi, CFSA, CRMA, *SoFi*

Joseph A. Mauriello, CIA, CFSA, CRMA, *University of Texas at Dallas*

Mark J. Pearson, CIA

Sundaresan Rajeswar, CIA, CCSA, CFSA, CGAP, CRMA, *Teyseer Group of Companies*

Bismark Rodriguez, CIA, CCSA, CFSA, CRMA, *Financial Services Risk Management*

Hesham K. Shawa, *IIA Jordon — International*

Deanna F. Sullivan, CIA, CRMA, *SullivanSolutions*

Jason Robert Thogmartin, CIA, CRMA, *Santander Holdings USA, Inc.*

Ashley R. Threeton, *ConocoPhillips*

Adriana Beatriz Toscano Rodriguez, CIA, CRMA, *UTE*

Jane Traub, CIA, CCSA, *The Nielsen Company*

Maritza Villanueva, CIA, *Regal Forest Holding*

Paul L. Walker, *St. John's University*

Larry G. Wallis, CIA, *VIA Metropolitan Transit*

Chance R. Watson, CIA, CRMA, *Texas Department of Family & Protective Services*

Klaas J. Westerling, CIA, *Intertrust Group Holding S.A.*